Please Accept Me

Please Accept Me

by

Thomas Cornwall

with

Judson Cornwall

Logos International
Plainfield, New Jersey

PLEASE ACCEPT ME
Copyright © 1979 by Logos International
All rights reserved
Printed in the United States of America
Library of Congress Catalog Card Number: 79-90401
International Standard Book Number: 0-88270-391-9
Logos International, Plainfield, New Jersey 07060

To all of my mentally retarded friends who, while accepting my instructions, have in turn taught me.

Contents

Preface

There is no way to document all the methods and theories being used today to train and teach the mentally retarded. There are many good programs in use, and with new understanding of the problems we face in the field of mental health, other new and workable programs will be developed.

This book chronicles one man's program that has proven to be successful.

The author wishes to show that there is often hope in seemingly hopeless situations and to portray the mentally retarded individual as a viable human being, deserving the same opportunities for living to his full potential as the rest of us. Mentally retarded persons are not God's rejects who somehow do not measure up to His standards. They are rejected by men because they are not understood and do not measure up to man's idea of normalcy. This book is my simple attempt to bring understanding to others, especially to the Christians of America, so that those who have been rejected may be received as potential brothers and sisters in Christ Jesus.

M.R. Does Not Mean "Mister"

The panic in her voice alerted me immediately. I knew something was wrong. Opening the door quickly, I found myself standing face to face with an agitated young lady who was on the verge of tears.

"What's wrong, Terri?" I asked. "Tell me."

"Well," she hesitantly said as she seated herself in the chair by my office door, "I really don't know where to start."

"Why don't you start at the beginning?" I suggested.

"Well," she said, obviously reaching for words, "you know I don't want to hurt anything, don't you?"

"Yes, of course. Go on, Terri."

"Well, I think I should tell you—it's pretty important—"

"Go on, go on," I said somewhat impatiently.

"Well—you see, I was ironing, and—"

The long pause while she sought the inner courage to continue was too much for me. "Yes, and what?" I prodded.

"Well, the iron cord burned out," she blurted out. Then she jumped up and opened the door to leave.

"Just a minute, Terri," I said. "These things happen; it was just the result of a lot of use. Nobody blames you for it. We can get it fixed tomorrow."

She relaxed momentarily and closed the door. Then she stood quickly and reopened it.

"That's not really the big trouble," she said, already standing halfway into the hallway while trying desperately to hold back the tears.

"Okay, then, what is the trouble, Terri?" I asked. But she never had a chance to answer, for my last words were interrupted by the staccato clanging of the fire alarm in the house. Bells were ringing on every floor of Hebron Home, a living and training center for mentally retarded persons. The noise of many feet running to the nearest exits created an instant mental picture of residents streaming from the fire exits of the house, repeating what they had learned and practiced so many times before during fire drills.

With a "Come on, Terri," I leaped up the stairs to the main floor and ran into a billowing cloud of smoke. Holding my breath, I pushed Terri out the front door and then ran through the three-story house, checking to see that all residents were safely evacuated. Quite obviously, the fire drills had been worthwhile, for every room was empty.

As I ran back to the kitchen area I saw a fireman pull a large plastic garbage can from a closet and empty his fire extinguisher into it.

"No flames," he said, "just a smoker."

Carefully picking through the now water-soaked contents, we found a still-hot iron. "Call Terri," I directed.

It took a bit of searching to locate her among the excited residents who were huddled together in the vacant lot next-door to the house, not too unlike a herd of sheep which had been threatened.

As she finally stepped into the kitchen, her eyes were as wide as saucers, and she obviously expected a reprimand.

"That's what I was trying to tell you," she said. "Well, when the cord burned in two I didn't think the iron was any good any more, so I put it in the garbage can and it started to smoke."

"Terri," I said, putting my arm around her shoulder, "let this be a lesson to you. Don't ever be afraid to tell someone exactly what you have in your mind. Don't worry about rejection or punishment. People will love you more if you say what you have to say."

"Looks like I goofed again," she sighed as she turned to leave. But I knew she had learned a lesson that would greatly help her to mature.

Terri isn't "crazy," or even mentally ill. She is retarded. She's a classic example of an M. R. individual. She is slow—very slow—to learn, experience, or express. But she does these things.

Mental retardation means impaired or incomplete mental development. The M.R. person's ability to learn, and his capacity to put that learning to use, is limited, but it is a limitation, not an absence of these capacities. Mental retardation involves the slowing down rather than the "stopping" of mental processes. Retarded persons think, feel hope, and love, just like everyone else, and although they have limitations, they have more similarities to other persons than differences.

The incidence of mental retardation is far more widespread than is commonly believed. The President's Commission on Mental Health reports that 25 percent of all Americans suffer from mental problems which include anxiety, emotional disorders, retardation, and chronic mental illness.

"Mental problems afflict almost all Americans," the report concluded—"either themselves, or in their families, or among their neighbors and friends. . . . the fear and misunderstanding of mental illness and emotional problems are deeply ingrained in our society."

But it is a mistake to classify retardation as a mental illness. Mental illness can be temporary, like many other types of illnesses, whereas mental retardation is usually a lifelong condition. Mental illness occurs most frequently in the early adult and later middle years of a person's life, but mental retardation occurs at or very near the birth experience. It is almost always recognized by school age.

Still another contrast is seen in the fact that mental illness does not necessarily interfere with strictly intellectual abilities and can often be cured by counseling, medication, or surgery. Mental retardation, on the other hand, is characterized by impaired intellectual development, and while it may be treated through educational techniques and therapy, it cannot be cured—short of a divine miracle.

The heartache of mental retardation is shared by many families in America, for a mentally retarded child is born every five minutes—a total of more than one hundred thousand per year. As many as one out of every thirty-five Americans could be classified as M.R. This is 3 percent of our population. The total cost of mental retardation in special services and lost wages is about $6 billion annually, but the cost of anxiety, grief, guilt feelings, heartache, shame, and emotional trauma is incalculable.

I have seen aging mothers who have devoted their entire lives to sheltering and caring for an M.R. child. Because they fear for the future of their loved one after they have died, they finally assign him or her to our home. While I feel a deep sympathy for the forty-year old M.R. who we accept into the home, I feel even more deeply for the guilt-ridden mother who has virtually thrown away her life caring for her deficient child. It is pity that I feel, for the fears, guilt, and shame that cause devoted mothers to withdraw from life are totally unnecessary and unfounded, and they actually prevent the M.R. from developing skills or abilities that would make him both acceptable and useful in the "normal" world. Every time this happens, two lives are wasted just because mental retardation is not understood.

But understanding retardation is not easy. For many years little or no research was done on mental retardation, but in recent years there has been a broad spectrum of research in the fields of biology, genetics, education, and psychology. Data has been compiled in graphs and charts to show the relationship of a father's occupation to a child's I.Q., the I.Q. of the mother as it relates to the mentally retarded, the percentage of M.R.s in various population conditions, and so forth. Each researcher pursues a new idea and compiles a different set of statistics.

Independent research will always produce diverse conclusions, but there seems to be a general agreement that 70 to 80 percent of persons who are identified as mentally retarded are the products of a subcultural family environment. There is a relationship between mental retardation and "cultural-familial environment." The discriminated-against minorities and the economically poor groups have a higher percentage of retarded individuals than do the white middle-class groups.

But obviously mental retardation is not confined to these groups, for there are various reasons for mental retardation, and there are M.R.s of all colors, races, cultures, and creeds. No segment of the American population or geography is exempt. Perhaps this malady is universal because over 250 specific causes for mental retardation have been identified, yet these account for less than one-half of all cases of mental retardation, since any condition, illness, or injury that interferes with mental development before, during or after birth can cause mental retardation. Heredity factors, genetic abnormalities, poor prenatal care, and chemical imbalances within the body are all responsible for mental retardation. It is also possible to become mentally retarded through lack of mental stimulation, or as a result of physical abuse, poverty, discrimination, and other nonmedical conditions.

Since there is no measurable damage to brain tissue itself, it is usually impossible to know beforehand if an infant will be mentally retarded or not.

While it may be argued that there are from two to three hundred possible causes for mental retardation, these can be reduced to eight leading ones:

1. *Infections during pregnancy*, especially in the first three months, may cause retardation. German measles (rubella) is one infectious disease that can cause a baby to be born with mental retardation, but this can be prevented by vaccination.

2. *Abnormal deliveries* contribute to mental retardation, for premature babies are more often retarded than are full-term babies. Very long, or extremely rapid, or even difficult childbirths can restrict the oxygen supply available to the infant (onoxia), thereby causing brain damage that leads to retardation.

3. *Infectious illness in infancy*, such as meningitis or encephalitis, may affect mental development unless diagnosed and treated early.

4. *Toxic agents* eaten or inhaled by the pregnant mother or the new baby can cause mental retardation. Lead poisoning from chewing lead-painted objects has been known to cause retardation. Federal restrictions in the use of lead-based paint on children's furniture has greatly reduced the incidence of mental retardation from this cause.

5. *Metabolic disorders*, or defects in the body chemistry, can cause several types of retardation. If diagnosed promptly, these forms of retardation can be corrected through medicine and proper diet.

6. *Rh blood factor incompatibility* may lead to severe retardation. Good prenatal care and transfusions right after birth can prevent damage. More recently, a series of vaccines has been produced for Rh-negative mothers which will prevent brain damage to the baby in many cases.

7. *Physical malformations* such as hydrocephalus (fluid accumulation in the brain) and craniosynostosis (premature hardening of the skull) sometimes result in mental retardation. Fortunately, these can sometimes be corrected by surgery.

8. *Down's syndrome*, a genetic defect we used to call Mongolism, affects one out of every six hundred, fifty babies born in the United States. It is more common when the mother is over thirty-five years old. There is no known cure.

Since mental retardation has so many causes, it is to be expected that it would be widespread, and that it would touch the lives of most of us in one way or another. We do well to remember that although it is incurable, it is not hopeless. Progress can be made toward normalcy if guidance and love can be administered in massive doses.

2

"I Never Could Tell Them Apart"

"How do you know he is Korean?" my brother Judson asked the missionary as they stood side by side on the streets of Sydney, Australia. "I can't tell the difference between a Taiwanese, Chinese, Japanese, or Korean person."

"When you've lived among them as long as I have," the missionary answered, "they don't look alike any more than they act alike. Each nationality seems to have physical and personality characteristics that are as different as their languages."

"But I can't even distinguish between their languages," Judson admitted. "They all sound alike to me; even their written language looks the same."

"That's because your ear isn't used to the different forms of speech, and your eye hasn't learned to read their character language. The differences are as pronounced as the difference between German and English."

Several months later when Judson was conducting a series of ministerial institutes in the Orient, a Korean pastor approached him and called him by the wrong name.

"I'm not Mr. Pritchard," my brother said. "I'm Judson Cornwall. Les Pritchard is on the other side of the platform."

"Please to forgive," the pastor apologized, "but I never could tell you Americans apart. During World War II the Japanese built a prisoner-of-war camp here in Pusan. My friends and I used to stand outside the barbed wire fence and watch the Americans, marveling that they could recognize one another, for we never learned to distinguish one from another, as you have just discovered. You all look alike to us."

How characteristic this is of life. As long as we stand outside the fence merely looking in, we will probably never be able to discern the differences between people, especially between the diverse levels of the mentally retarded. To merely lump all mentally handicapped individuals under the simplistic heading of "mentally retarded" is about as descriptive as calling all residents of the Orient "Orientals," or all white people "Caucasians." While the terms are accurate, they are far too broad to be descriptive.

Every parent has learned that children are as different as they are alike, and all who have worked with the mentally retarded have learned similarly. It is grossly unfair to label them as "two peas in a pod," for often they are as unlike as a carrot and a beet.

Until the middle of the twentieth century, degrees of retardation were indicated by such terms as idiot, imbecile, moron, or dull-witted. In England and some European countries the terms backward or subnormal were common. Slowly these terms gave way to the more modern categories of mild, moderate, severe, or profound retardation; or, as some professionals prefer to catalogue them, the educable, trainable, and severely retarded.

This helped to differentiate between various types of retardation and perhaps made observations more accurate and assistance better tailored to the need, but these terms deal only with degrees of retardation. They do not adequately define it, if in fact an adequate definition can be found. Consider some of the more recent attempts to define mental retardation.

The National Association for Retarded Children (NARC) defines mental retardation as "a condition in which intelligence is prevented from attaining full development, limiting the victim's ability to learn and put learning to use." The National Institutes of Neurological Diseases and Blindness (NINDB) offer this definition: "Mental retardation is a condition in which an individual, by reason of intellectual inadequacy, is incapable of performing at the level required for acceptable adjustment within his cultural environment." In another place they simply define mental retardation as "a manifestation of disease or dysfunction of the brain." The Children's Bureau of the Department of Health, Education and Welfare calls mental retardation "impaired or incomplete mental development."

In her book, *Mentally Retarded Children*, Harriet E. Blodgett writes, "Mental retardation is defined as inadequate intelligence. But just what is intelligence? In down-to-earth terms, one might say it means the ability to exercise common sense—knowing enough to come in out of the rain, being able to meet new problems and solve them. A more professional definition would refer to the capacity to think abstractly and make use of symbols."[1]

Usually the professionals measure the mental capacity of individuals to determine their intelligence quotient (IQ, as it is commonly called). The highest possible score is 200. The average person ranges from 90 to 110; the borderline person or slow learner has an IQ of about 80-90, while scores in the lower range between 0 and 70 indicate mental retardation. But surely mental retardation is more than a score on a test. The American Association for Mental Deficiency's definition for mental retardation is "subaverage general intellectual functioning which originates during the developmental period (conception to seventeen years) and is associated with impairment in adaptive behavior."

Richard Koch, M.D., says, "The mentally retarded person is one who has suffered an impairment of his ability to think, learn and reason. The cause of this impairment may have occurred at the time he was conceived, during the period of gestation, during the birth process, or during his infancy or childhood. The cause may be known, but more often it is not. It may be a hereditary condition, or it may merely be an unfortunate accident of nature. While mental retardation can occur in a wide range of severity, it is nearly always a chronic disorder which cannot be cured in the usual sense but whose effects can often be minimized."

The Children's Bureau of HEW also declares, "At any age, an accident to the brain, or an inflammation or contagious disease, or a brain tumor can leave damage to the brain resulting in mental retardation. However, most biological causes do their damage before, during, or soon after birth—which is the so-called 'perinatal period.' "

But, as Glenn Doman, director of the Institutes for the Achievement of Human Potential, points out, "Referring to brain injury as mental retardation would be much the same as referring to appendicitis as fever and a pain in the lower abdominal area." It would seem that a more proper diagnostic term for these children would be "brain-injured."

These varied and somewhat diverse definitions seem to indicate that the term "mental retardation" is more a description of a condition or conditions than it is a diagnosis. It seems that the true meaning of the term has not been agreed upon. Nonetheless, we do recognize that mental retardation refers to a slowdown in mental processes.

In Blodgett's book, referred to earlier, the author states, "The degree of a child's retardation forecasts his rate of mental growth and determines within some variations his final limit. One analogy that may clarify this is to compare mental growth with different modes of transportation. A gifted child would be like a jet plane which crosses the continent in a few hours. The normal, average child is like a propeller-type plane that flies not quite coast to coast and takes longer. The educable child is a passenger train that stops at many towns and only runs for four hundred miles. The trainable child is more like a freight train which covers sixty miles at a very slow rate. When we talk about degrees of retardation, we are dealing with differences in speed and with differences in ultimate destination. The more severe the retardation, the earlier mental growth slows up and levels off, so that trainable children reach their final mental maturity earlier than educable children, who in turn reach their final level of mental maturity earlier than normal children."[2]

Beatrice Buckler sheds more light on these degrees of retardation when she writes, "Mentally retarded youngsters fall into three major categories:

"The *educable retarded*, also known as the mildly retarded, grow up to be adults who are limited intellectually but who nonetheless can work at simple jobs and are able to assume normal family responsibilities. They are content to do work others might find dull, and they are able to live self-supporting lives within this category. With seventy-five out of one hundred in this category, they make up the majority of mentally handicapped children.

"The *trainable retarded* may be able to work in sheltered workshops but need general supervision with others providing a home for them throughout their lives. Within a sheltered situation, some can be partly self-supporting.

"The *severely retarded* require supervision and care throughout their lives, although when given sufficient opportunities in childhood they, too, can make surprisingly good progress."[3]

So, obviously, M.R.s are not all alike. There are at least four specific categories with degrees of variation in each grouping. In learning to work with the mentally retarded, we use a quick-reference chart that reviews some of the major differences between levels of retardation.

Before IQ tests were devised, people were generally classified by their personality traits, or behavior characteristics, which often proved disastrous. Perhaps some retarded persons were put to death by our Puritan forefathers as witches, for the records indicate that anyone appearing or acting a little "different" came

DEVELOPMENTAL CHARACTERISTICS

Degree of Retardation	Pre-School (0-5 years)	School Age (6-12 years)	Adult (21 and over)
MILD (Educable) I.Q. 53-67 89% of all M.R.s	Often not diagnosed until later age.	Learns academic and prevocational skills with some special training.	Lives and works in the community. May not be easily identified as retarded.
MODERATE (Trainable) I.Q. 36-52 6% of all M.R.s	Fair motor development. Can learn to talk and care for personal needs.	Learns functional academic skills. Can be independent in familiar surroundings.	Performs semi-skilled work under sheltered conditions.
SEVERE I.Q. 21-35 3½% of all M.R.s	Slow motor development; some communication skills. May have physical handicaps.	Can talk or learn to talk; cares for personal needs.	Can contribute to self-maintenance with supervision in work and living situations.
PROFOUND I.Q. 20- 1½% of all M.R.s	Minimal overall responsiveness. Often has secondary physical handicaps.	Slow motor development. Can be taught some basic self-care skills.	Some communication skills. Cares for basic needs. Some highly structured work activities.

under immediate suspicion.

Koch tells us, "The advent of 'hospitals' and asylums for the mentally incompetent coincided with the cessation of witch-hunting. The first hospital for the mentally ill in the United States was built in Williamsburg, Virginia, in 1773. These asylums were more like prisons than hospitals, where the poor victims were chained in tiny cells without heat or proper food. And some of the medical treatments used to try to cure them were little better than the tortures used to gain confessions from witches in earlier years."[4]

I have often wondered how many mentally competent persons who suffered from epilepsy or who had rather extreme personality characteristics finished out their lives in these asylums, for it is human nature to see ourselves as the standard "norm" and to judge others' behavior accordingly. Still, we know that a different personality is not, in itself, either inferior or superior to ours.

I have come to recognize that there are as many personality differences in mentally retarded persons as there are in "normal" persons. In 1964, Professor Rick Heber, in his *Research of Personality Disorders*, said, "Despite the generally acknowledged importance of personality factors in problem solving, there has been little experimental work relative to personality development and characteristics of the retarded. Not one of such commonly purported attributes of the retarded, such as passivity, anxiety, impulsivity, rigidity, suggestibility, a lack of persistence, immaturity, withdrawal, low frustration tolerance, unrealistic self-concept or level of aspiration, can be either substantiated or refuted on the basis of research data."[5]

Although this is changing, it is a fact that research in the personality area in mental retardation is still in its infancy. As Dr. Heber suggests, there remain many misconceptions about the personality characteristics of the M.R., and these misconceptions are prevalent even among those in the behavioral and social sciences.

I presume that one of the reasons for this is the common assumption that the M.R. is subnormal, not only in his (or her) learning characteristics, but in most other areas of his psychological characteristics as well. Since he is subnormal in his learning abilities, his behavior is viewed as simple, fixed, rigid and relatively unchangeable. But this is not so. The behavior of the retarded can be changed—sometimes to an astonishing extent. The behavior patterns of an M.R. child are flexible and trainable, although it may take more effort and patience to effect that training than it does with a normal child.

"But is it only the behavior pattern of the M.R. that can be changed?" I began asking.

"Basically, yes," I was told. "Since retardation is irreversible, you should not expect to effect cures, so don't raise false hopes or expectations."

This point of view seemed far too hopeless. If

an M.R. person was to be forever locked into a specific category on the chart, then it seemed senseless to work so hard with him. But I remembered reading the Gottesman and Shield study on intelligence quotients, which notes that environmental factors can make a difference of fourteen IQ points. If a change of environment could actually raise intelligence that much, what would patient, loving, Christian caring do? And what about training? Could a near-hopeless M.R. be raised to a higher level where his life would be useful to others instead of being completely dependent upon others? Lily proved to me that it really could.

I had almost forgotten about Lily, for it had been nearly a year since I had seen her—a very busy year for me. Her voice on the phone sounded confident and happy as she said, "Mr. Cornwall, I just wanted you to know that since I left Hebron Home I have fallen in love and have married a wonderful man. Things are going real well for us, too. Thank you for believing in me and for helping me learn how to be a useful person."

"And her parents thought she was a hopeless case," I mused to myself. I reached into the files to reread Lily's entrance questionnaire.

"If she can boil water without scorching the pan, I will be surprised," the mother had written.

Lily was thirty-four years old then and had lived in the seclusion of her parents' home all of her life. Because she was obviously retarded, her folks didn't know she could learn anything, so they had never given her the opportunity to be exposed to learning situations.

"What a shame it is," I thought, "that just because a retarded person is slower at learning a task than his nonretarded peers, he is often denied the opportunity to develop the talents he does possess."

This was Lily's problem. We had determined to at least give her the chance to develop her potential, so we welcomed her into Hebron Home with open arms. Since the homelike surroundings were similar to what she was used to, the change was not too threatening to her. What was different was being with others who had problems similar to hers, for all of the residents were M.R.s. But Lily seemed to be more handicapped than the rest, for she wasn't even self-supporting in the areas of her personal care.

Among the first lessons Lily had to master was personal hygiene. The staff worked long and hard to try to instill in her a sense of self-worth by encouraging her to wear clean clothes of styles that were consistent with her age. She wasn't a little girl any more and shouldn't dress like it.

I also remembered how patiently the staff demonstrated the use of cosmetics, and taught her to fix her own hair. These teaching sessions were balanced with frequent and friendly counseling sessions. We almost had to teach her to communicate, for although she could talk, she had never been encouraged to express her thoughts and deep feelings.

After many months of work with Lily, there was a marked change in her outward appearance and in her ability to relate to the others in the home. Still, Lily had a "lost" look in her eyes and her behavior was antagonistic, especially to the housemother on the staff. Often, seemingly for no apparent reason, she would become extremely defensive and belligerent, and occasionally she became physically violent if she was not granted her own way.

After many hours of counseling, Lily finally trusted me enough to share some of her inner conflicts and problems that had been hidden in her thoughts for many years. As best as her vocabulary and emotions would permit, she related, "It's all my mother's fault. She made me this way. I hate her!"

The cascading tears, the set jaw, and the clenched fist revealed how deeply she actually felt this to be true.

Breathing a quick prayer to God for guidance, I reached for my Bible and began to read to her, explaining from the portions I had felt led to read that none of us needs to keep hatred, resentment, bitterness, and anger bottled up inside of us, for this will only make us sick. In words she could comprehend, and with much tenderness and love, I showed her that Jesus can take away our hatred and give us love in its place. I encouraged her to give her mind over to Jesus for healing and to ask Him for a new heart and personality.

She responded very positively and, at my suggestion, she phoned her mother and asked forgiveness for the way she had felt toward her.

I don't remember that there was an instantaneous change in Lily, but notes in her file indicate that she began giving more attention to the other residents of the home—helping with little things. There was, however, an almost immediate change for the better in her attitude toward the staff and in her approach to her studies.

Because of this, we established a long-range goal for her to get a high school diploma. It was a laborious task for her that consumed most of her time for a couple of years, but she achieved it. How proud she was when that diploma was finally awarded! That wasn't all, for she also earned a cooking certificate from the home, which attested that she had cooked three separate meals—breakfast, lunch and supper— for the entire home. Yet her mother hadn't believed she was capable of boiling water!

Recognizing the development in Lily, we encouraged her to get a job at a local restaurant. She was promoted from dishwasher to part-time cook within six months. She also did housework as a part-time job.

Lily left the home after three years to live in

her own apartment, and although she came in for weekly counseling for an additional year, she was finally on her own.

Oh, yes! Her mother became her best friend.

Now she phones me to let me know she is happily married. What a reward for four years of intensive involvement!

Lily illustrates the severe danger of not believing that an M.R. can move up the IQ charts. She who had been such a burden to her parents for thirty-four years is now self-sufficient and capable of offering love, tenderness, and care for another.

Is Lily's case unique? No! Our files contain the stories of many other Lilys. Ignorance of the peculiar problems of mental retardation has kept far too many from having the opportunity to step up the ladder toward normalcy. But Americans are awakening to this terrible waste of life. We're beginning to learn how to "comfort the mentally retarded."

3

Comfort the Retarded

For years Sunday school students have memorized the Ten Commandments given to Moses and the eight Beatitudes given by Jesus, but seldom are they challenged to learn the twelve exhortations of Paul as recorded in 1 Thessalonians 5:14-22. This is the passage which beseeches the Christian to "rejoice evermore"; "pray without ceasing"; "in everything give thanks"; and "quench not the Spirit." These exhortations are sung, soliloquized, and sermonized repeatedly, but I have never heard anyone start at the beginning of the list, for Paul did not call for perpetual rejoicing until he had urged the saints to "comfort the feeble minded, support the weak, be patient toward all men" (1 Thessalonians 5:14). He seemed to feel that true love will manifest itself first toward our brothers and sisters and then will naturally rise to God. (See Matthew 25:36 for Jesus' view on this.)

John said about the same thing when he wrote, "He that loveth not his brother whom he hath seen, how can he love God whom he hath not seen?" (1 John 4:20).

In exhorting us to "comfort the feeble minded," Paul uses the Greek word *oligopsuchos*, which is translatable as "feeble-minded, small-souled, despondent, or fainthearted." Certainly this would encompass the mentally retarded, for their basic problem is that they are "small-souled," or mentally underdeveloped. Because of this lack of mental sharpness, they are often rejected by society, overprotected by loved ones, and misunderstood by those who associate with them. This in itself could bring on despondency and faintheartedness.

Paul says that the church in general and the saints in particular have a responsibility to comfort the mentally retarded. He had set the example, for he said, "Ye know how we exhorted and comforted and charged every one of you, *as a father doth* his children, that ye would walk worthy of God" (1 Thessalonians 2:11, 12, emphasis added). This is the way he would have us comfort the M.R.—"as a father doth his children."

It is not "sloppy agape" that the M.R. needs; it is father-love with its incumbent training, encouragement, correction, example, exhortation, and approval. Comfort comes out of caring—genuine caring, concerned caring, involved caring!

James warned against trying to comfort with

words alone. He said, "If a brother or sister be naked, and destitute of daily food, and one of you say unto them, Depart in peace, be ye warmed and filled; notwithstanding ye give them not those things which are needful to the body; what doth it profit?" (James 2:15, 16).

Love is not merely an attitude. It is an action. Love gives what is needed. Love seldom needs to be told what to do; it sees the need and quickly moves to meet that need. Love doesn't require an organization to work through; it simply goes to work.

The mentally retarded need this love of Christians—a love that doesn't hesitate to touch or speak; a love that is willing to get involved; a love that is willing to accept the M.R. as he is, where he is, and for what he is.

It is not "comfort" to be talked down to, to be treated as a child, or to be merely accommodated. The M.R. needs to be received as a person, loved as an individual, and treated as a human being. Christian love can do this without forcing behavior responses beyond the M.R.'s ability. Agape love can receive the M.R. without setting up unachievable goals while assisting him or her to set and achieve reasonable goals. Patricia is a valid example of this.

"Excuse me, Mr. Cornwall," she said. "I would like to vacuum and dust your office before I prepare lunch for the home."

The housekeeper's words brought a smile to

my face, for my mind flashed back three years to my first meeting with Patricia. Accompanied by her mother, she had sat in this very same office, withdrawn, head bowed, and shaking with fright.

"She's been at home most of her life," her mother said. "She makes such a mess of anything she tries to do that we have just done everything for her. We deeply love our little girl and would gladly do anything for her. That's why we've brought her to Hebron Home. Maybe you can get her involved in something that will somehow bring her out of herself."

"What skills has she been able to develop up to this point?" I asked.

"She can take care of her personal hygiene, but that's about all," the mother replied.

Turning my attention away from the overly protective and obviously guilt-ridden mother, I took a good look at Patricia. Mama's "little girl" was twenty-four years old, but she dressed, sat, and acted like a five-year-old. I smiled at this lonesome and seemingly helpless girl and took her hand in mine. She seemed to be surprised, but she made no attempt to withdraw her hand.

"Look at me," I said gently. "Look right into my eyes and listen to what I am going to tell you."

With some hesitation she gradually raised her head and gazed directly into my eyes.

"God has given this home great love," I said. "We have plenty of it, and we want to share it with you. Do you know what that means?"

There was no answer to the question, but she kept looking right into my eyes, and I knew she was listening to me.

"Love is caring, and we care for you. I don't mean we will take care of you; I mean we will care enough about you to help you grow up in your mind and actions to match your twenty-four-year-old body."

The mother shifted uncomfortably as if to intervene and protect her daughter from false hopes, but I continued to speak, refusing to give her a point where she could interrupt me.

Still looking deep into Patricia's eyes, I said, "Before too long you will be able to read and write letters. You will learn to cook and sew like the other women; and one day, in the near future, you will be working on your own job, making money to buy clothes and other things. Patricia, would you like that?"

It probably sounded too good to be true, for she lowered her eyes to break contact with me, but the tear that ran down her right cheek gave evidence of her deep desire to achieve these very goals.

Because life at Hebron Home is lived so differently from the lives these people experienced in their private homes or institutions, we have a standing rule that a new resident cannot have visitors or outside phone calls for the first six weeks. This allows him orientation time without the conflict of reminders and emotional involvements with the past. Generally the new resident makes a healthy adjustment by the middle of the second month and is eager for relatives to visit so he can display his newly acquired skills.

The day her mother was scheduled to visit the home, Patricia was dressed up in a new outfit and was holding her reading study book on her lap when her mother arrived. It was a happy, although tearful, reunion.

"I never once thought Patricia could learn to read," her mother said as Patricia finished reading a simple Bible story to her.

"Mentally retarded people can do most of the things anyone else can do," I told her. "It usually takes longer to teach them, and you must be very patient with them. Please don't feel guilty about the way you raised Patricia. Like many parents of retarded children, you really didn't understand. You kept Patricia your 'little girl' too long, but now she is starting to grow. She needs a love that will let her grow, not a love that prevents her growth. That's where we can help best."

Now, three years later, Patricia has just finished cleaning the home and making lunch for the entire family before heading out to her afternoon jobs. She takes care of an invalid widow's home and does housekeeping and cooking for a working mother. She is almost self-supporting already, having "graduated" from the Hebron Home cooking classes with honors, thus making it possible for her to be promoted out of the group living situation to share a home with a foster mother and a roommate.

How is it possible to effect such changes in retarded persons? It is by tender, patient love that cares enough to get involved in teaching them to do at least one thing that has always been done for them, and then adding to that accomplishment still another skill.

Most retarded persons have been coddled and made to feel completely worthless. When we let them know someone cares whether they "grow up" or not, and then give them the education at the rate they can respond to, administered with large doses of agape love, something happens! Patricia is not so much an exception as many people would like to believe. Of course, if we had encouraged her to try for a degree in engineering or teaching, it would only have enlarged her frustration level, for this would have been beyond her capability levels.

When our love is willing to help M.R. individuals establish lesser goals and to assist them in attaining them, these people can become active citizens of the community, participating in most of the activities of society. Instead of being our burden, they become our brothers. It is basically a matter of magnifying what they can do instead of concentrating on what they cannot do.

The grasping of number concepts and the ability to read are the most important goals for the mentally retarded. Once they learn these skills, even to a limited degree, they are able to shop at stores and engage in varied kinds of employment. Since this is so, aren't the M.R.s worth a little investment of concerned love? Can't the Church use some of its time and energy to "comfort the feeble minded" by getting involved with them? It will mean meeting them at their point of need, but this is what Jesus meant when He said, "Come, ye blessed of my Father, inherit the kingdom prepared for you from the foundation of the world: For I was an hungred, and ye gave me meat: I was thirsty, and ye gave me drink: I was a stranger, and ye took me in: Naked, and ye clothed me: I was sick, and ye visited me: I was in prison, and ye came unto me. Inasmuch as ye have done it unto one of the least of these my brethren, ye have done it unto me" (Matthew 25:34-36, 40).

When I realize how rapidly these M.R.s respond to God's love, and what corrective therapy it becomes for them, I just want to shout to the whole Church, "Love them as though you were loving Christ himself. I love them with Christ's love. I love them sufficiently to be willing to give some of myself to them, and it is working miracles in their lives. They can be comforted if we will love them enough to become fathers and mothers to them and will patiently and lovingly instruct them in the basic patterns of life. They are not rejects; they are mentally

retarded, but they can catch up at least part way
if we will be willing to back up and show them the
way."

4

Spirit Is Not Soul

"Can my mentally retarded son be born again?" he asked, leaning forward in his chair as though he should whisper the question across the desk. "My wife and I worry about this constantly."

With that, he sank back into the upholstered chair, crossed his legs in a rapid manner, and nervously rubbed his lips with his left hand. His brow was furrowed, and his eyes stared at the floor.

"My Percy doesn't understand very much," he continued, "and communicates in single-syllable words, grunts, and gestures. We've read Bible stories to him and talked much about Jesus, but there just doesn't seem to be any response. I am afraid he doesn't understand enough to be saved."

Having said it aloud, he lifted his eyes to meet mine. He had the look of a man who had just confessed a long-hidden sin, for shame, anxiety, and fear with just a little glimmer of relief were mirrored in his eyes. For a brief moment I felt more like a father-confessor than the director of Hebron Home.

"Is your son an M.R. or an S.R.?" I asked him.

"I'm afraid I don't know what you mean by S.R.," he responded.

"I'm asking you if your son is mentally retarded or spiritually retarded," I continued.

"Well," he said, "Percy is obviously mentally retarded—quite severely, as a matter of fact, and I have always assumed this would automatically restrict his spiritual development. Doesn't it?"

While neither Percy nor his father are actual people, they represent a composite of many parents and their M.R. children, for this scenario has been repeated in my office time and time again. Christian parents are tormented with the fear that their retarded children cannot be saved because they cannot grasp theological concepts, take a catechism class, function in a Sunday school or church setting, or whatever. While we glibly quote, "For by grace are ye saved through faith; and that not of yourselves: it is the gift of God" (Ephesians 2:8), we actually associate various actions, attitudes, and emotional responses with our salvation experience. Somehow we seem to feel that what we did, felt, thought, or said contributed to our being born again. But salvation is a gift, not a reward; it is something we receive, not something we perceive. It is an action of God's Spirit upon our spirits, not God's mind upon our minds. God's B.A. is not a college degree; it is a new birth—we are born again of the Spirit of God. This process is entirely of God and is neither assisted nor thwarted by the individual's mental capacity.

The Bible says, "With the heart [not the head] man believeth unto righteousness" (Romans 10:10). The capacity to accept love is actually all that is required for a true born-again experience, and I have found M.R.s to be highly developed in this area of life. Whatever limitations they may have in their concepts and in relating to life, they are highly sensitive to and needy of love. That is why love therapy works so well. If their natural life can be positively altered by responding to love motivation, why would they have any difficulty in accepting and responding to God's love?

I have observed that quite the opposite is true. Because they have few of the inhibitions that hinder the "normal" adult from receiving from God on a Spirit-to-spirit level, I have found it easier to lead an M.R. to Christ than a college student. Let me tell you how this worked with Clara.

Clara weighed 263 pounds when she first enrolled at Hebron Home, and still she ate as though she would never see food again. When she wasn't eating, she was sleeping. She had lived eighteen of her twenty-eight years of life in a state hospital for the mentally retarded, and during all of those years she had learned merely to brush her teeth, tie her shoes, dress herself, and bathe when told to do so. Although repeated attempts had been made to teach her to read, the most she had learned were a few emergency words such as stop, go, exit, and so forth. Clara did not have a family and had few friends.

Her food-spattered dress, stretched far too tightly over her obese body, added nothing positive to her appearance as she walked awkwardly with a heavy step toward her new home. We had accepted Clara on a thirty-day trial basis to see if she could relate favorably to the family-type living arrangement at Hebron Home.

Most of the family simply ignored Clara as she backed up to one of the overstuffed chairs in the living room and literally dropped her weight into the groaning chair. But eventually one of the family of seventeen persons walked over to Clara, stood in front of her and eyed her from head to toe. "Why are you so fat?" she asked in an open and noncondemning manner.

"Because I like to eat," Clara answered. "When is supper served here?"

While this innocent interaction was underway, I noticed one of my skill-trainers writing notes furiously. Peeking over her shoulder, I read, "Training schedule: cooking."

"Why not?" I exclaimed. "She would be a natural for working in the kitchen, with her love for food."

Clara responded to family life beautifully, and at the end of the first month was accepted as a permanent resident. We put her on a diet that restricted her intake of food to 750 calories a day, explaining to her that because of our love for her we couldn't let her abuse her body through overeating. We used an incentive program that offered short-term goals which were easily attained. Small monthly awards took much of the pain out of dieting. We also hung an expensive dress, many sizes too small, near her dresser and frequently spoke of how exciting it would be for her to wear it. All awards and compliments were given with a hug and kiss, and all restrictions were given while we had a loving touch contact with her.

Her potential as a cook developed very rapidly, and before long Clara was cooking meals for the entire family with only a minimum of supervision. In spite of her close association with food she stayed on her diet until she was down to a healthy 154 pounds by the end of the year.

She also began to excel in her home studies, and after some time she could read most of the Bible with acceptable comprehension.

One morning her Bible reading was in the third chapter of John, where she read of God's self-giving love in verse 16. Stopping me as I walked through the room, she asked, "Do you love me enough to die for me, like Jesus did?"

This took me by surprise, and I faltered for a moment before answering, "I might die for a few close friends, but Jesus died for millions of people He didn't even know. Most of the people who Jesus died for had not even been born when He went to the cross at Calvary, but He still loved them."

"If He really loved me so much," she responded, "I want to love Him, too." Without fanfare, altar call, emotional expression, or further explanation, Clara accepted Jesus as her Lord and Savior. She merely responded to His love—first as it had been shown to her by staff members, and then as she had seen it in God's Word. Her life subsequently bore fruit that revealed the genuineness of her conversion.

Abnormal? Unusual? Unique? No! The mentally retarded are not automatically spiritually retarded. The defect in their soul (mind) does not mean there will be a defect in their spirit (the God-conscious portion in mankind).

My brother Judson, co-author of this book, pastored churches for more than twenty-five years. He always had a compassionate heart for the mentally retarded and always had several of them in every church he pastored. I well remember his telling me that the spiritual maturity of individuals was not tied to their mental capacity, and that he had observed deep spiritual experiences in the lives of M.R.s and always approached them as spiritually mature in spite of their obvious social and mental immaturity. When God's Spirit interacted with their spirits, there was no discernible limitation. Gifts of the Spirit flowed through them occasionally, and the fruit of the Spirit could be seen in them regularly.

"Do you think they understand your sermons?" I asked him one day.

"Not likely," he said with a twinkle in his eye, "for sometimes I wonder if even I understand them.

"But while they may not be able to intellectually comprehend spiritual truths," he added, "they certainly are aware of the presence of the Lord in the service and are quick to respond to the anointing of the Spirit in the sermon."

"Aren't they just reacting to the emotional surge of the service?" I asked.

"No," he said. "Although they seem ready to respond to emotional stimuli faster than many others do, I believe the Holy Spirit within them responds to the truth that is preached and impresses it upon their spirits. Just as we are often aware of knowing something in our spirits that we cannot express through our mouths, so they gain knowledge in their spirits that they are unable to filter down through their conscious minds. But their spirits are profited, and mature and develop in spite of the mental handicap."

"So you honestly believe that the spirit of a man can act independently of his soul?" I asked, looking beyond my brother at the rocky mountain crag just outside his hotel room.

"Of course," he answered. "While the spirit and soul interact and are mutually dependent upon the body for expression in the physical world, it is the spirit that acts as the throne room—not the soul. The control of life is in man's spirit once he has surrendered himself to the lordship of Christ. I developed this quite fully in chapter five of my book *Let Us Abide*."[6]

"I know," I said, "and I have reread that chapter several times, but I never associated it with M.R.s."

Neither of us spoke for a few minutes as we took time to peel a banana and enjoy a snack. I got up from my place on the sofa and walked to the window. A children's camp was in progress at the same time my brother's convention was being held on these conference grounds, and from the third floor I could see the children in excited play as they headed for the swimming pool.

"I suppose it is very much like those children," I said, to break the silence. "They have so very much to learn, and yet they have been able to accept the love of their parents and friends even though they would be hard pressed to define love. More than that, many of them have had true conversion experiences."

"I was only three years old when I was soundly born again," Judson said, "and you were saved in your grammar school days. How much theology did we understand?"

"I know," I said. "But do we have any scriptural basis for saying that a person's spirit can respond to God even if the intellect of the soul is greatly restricted?"

"How about John the Baptist?" he asked. "While he was still in his mother's womb, Mary, who was pregnant with Jesus, visited their home in Judea. As soon as Mary greeted Elizabeth, John the Baptist leaped in his mother's womb and was filled with the Holy Spirit."

"Where does it say that?" I queried.

"In Luke 1:41," he replied. "Even to this day, scientists do not have evidence that the conscious mind or emotions (the soul) of the embryo function at all. Still, John the Baptist was declared to be 'filled with the Spirit' while he was still in the womb with an undeveloped, or totally inactive, soul."

"That's a greater mental incapacity than I've ever tried to treat," I said. "I guess I'll never meet an M.R. who can't be saved."

"You might be further encouraged to know," Judson added, "that I have led completely unconscious persons into salvation. Although their souls could not respond, their spirits could, and they later testified to having understood everything I said to them and had responded as I had asked them to respond. I think we have placed too great an emphasis on the action of the natural mind in embracing God's salvation. The Bible places the emphasis upon the believing of the 'heart' or spirit of man."

I programed this information in the memory circuits of my mind's computer, hoping to be able to recall it rapidly enough in the future to offer hope and assurance to the next parent who expressed genuine fear over his mentally retarded child's ability to respond to God's great saving love as it is expressed in the person of Jesus Christ. Since salvation is in a Person, not a doctrine, anyone who can accept the Person of Jesus Christ and embrace His love can be saved. If, as Robert Rakes, the founder of the Sunday school, used to say, "It is as natural for a child to turn to God as it is for the morning glory to turn to the sun," then these M.R.s, who seem to live in perpetual childhood, should enter into saving grace more naturally than the "sophisticated" unbeliever.

"Suffer the little children to come unto me, and forbid them not," Jesus said, "for of such is the kingdom of God" (Mark 10:14). I have found that if the M.R. can receive me and my love, he is capable of receiving Christ and His love.

5

"I Deserve Punishment"

Perhaps it is human nature to magnify our differences more than our similarities. Certainly this seems to be true when we encounter a retarded person. Most of our withdrawal from them is rooted in our fear of their differences from us, and we often assume they are vastly unlike us in every way. We fail to recognize that they have the same emotions, desires, and social needs we have. Their inability to aptly vocalize feelings does not mean they are without feelings. An incapacity in motor ability does not indicate a lack of pride in accomplishment. Although they may become confused with the rituals of our church, this is not evidence that they lack spiritual perception or religious desires.

Perhaps one of the greatest fallacies I have heard expressed repeatedly is, "The retarded are such innocent children. They don't know right from wrong." Don't you believe it! Guilt from wrongdoing plagues the retarded as surely as it haunts the rest of us. The divinely built-in conscience is not deactivated just because the mind is limited in its functions. The retarded have to learn how to handle guilt or they will suffer the consequences just like the rest of us. Their code of right and wrong may differ from ours somewhat just as ours may differ from those of other cultures, but the penalty of guilt is very real to them. They do not see themselves as innocents. The truth of Romans 3:23 is very real to them: "All have sinned and come short of the glory of God."

If the Christians shy away from communicating with them, and the church rejects them, what are the M.R.s to do with their load of guilt?

Dawn came up with her own answer to the pressure of subdued guilt. "Do you really believe God forgives us for every wrong we have ever done?" she asked me for well over the hundredth time that year.

Perhaps the constant repetition of the query should have alerted me to the depth of her inner conflict, but she always seemed to accept my assurance of God's love.

Dawn is not only a mentally retarded person; she also has emotional problems which stem from the difficulty she has had in adjusting to society. A load of guilt for something done in the past compounds her problems. It was something done probably in her youth, that she has been unable to forgive, forget, or receive forgiveness for.

I well remember my first encounter with Dawn. Shortly after her entry into Hebron Home she began to withdraw and become morose. Although her behavior wasn't too distracting to the other residents in the home, she constantly sought praise and acceptance. A few weeks after her trial-stay period was over, one of the staff reported that Dawn was limping. Upon examination, we discovered her left knee was badly swollen and inflamed.

"Did you fall down?" I asked her.

"No," she answered.

"Did you twist your leg?" I persisted in my questioning.

"No," she replied rather stoically.

"Do you know what happened to your knee to make it so sore?" I asked. There was no answer.

At the doctor's office the same questions got the same responses, so x-rays were taken of the knee. After reading the pictures, the doctor called me into his office and said, "Mr. Cornwall, there is a foreign object under Dawn's kneecap. It looks like a sewing needle."

Calling Dawn into the office with us, I confronted her with the photographic evidence and again asked her what had happened, but she professed ignorance as to how the needle could possibly have gotten there. Fortunately, the eye of the needle had not gone completely under the kneecap, enabling the doctor to remove it without surgery.

In the many weeks that followed, Dawn continued to refuse to discuss the mystery needle.

About six months later we had a repeat performance, but this time it was in the opposite knee; and this time she had successfully pushed the entire needle under the kneecap, requiring an operation to remove the needle.

It was while she was undergoing the surgery that I began to put two and two together. She had repeatedly asked me if her past was truly forgiven, but somehow my answers didn't satisfy her. This overt action of needles under the kneecaps was a form of penance she was doing for the guilt she was carrying around in her conscience.

When I pursued this line of reasoning with her she readily admitted the self-flagellation. "I deserve to be punished," she said with great emotion.

When our counselors were able to show her how to remit her sins to Christ through confession and repentance, and how to accept His forgiveness, she subsequently forgave herself and the self-punishment ceased.

I cannot help wondering how many Dawns there are across the nation. The Christians may extend themselves to say, "Jesus loves you and I love you," but M.R.s need someone to show them how to unburden their hearts and minds of the heavy weight of guilt. It is hard for the guilty to accept proffered love from the judge who will eventually sentence them to death. They must know Jesus as Savior before they can accept Him as their lover. They, as all of us, need to find and live in forgiveness before God's love has very much meaning. I have found if they can be conscious of sin they can also be made aware of forgiveness, and subsequently they can learn to live as forgiven persons.

Christian mothers long ago learned how to bring their children to the cross of Christ for forgiveness. May God cause today's Christians to use that knowledge to bring the childlike persons to Jesus, first for forgiveness and then for a flow of Christ's love. They should not have to live with a sense of "I deserve punishment."

I have lived too long to suggest that all guilty M.R.s will participate in self-flagellation, for guilt produces as many varied responses in them as it does in anyone else. But whatever the response, if guilt is its cause, only forgiveness will change the behavior.

Grandma Roberts was also a victim of guilt, but she would never have pushed a needle under her kneecap. That just wasn't consistent with her nature. In fact, I doubt if she would have been capable of such an act because of her great fear of almost everything in life. Fear completely controlled Grandma, and thereby limited her participation in life.

One of the most immobilizing forces in life is fear. It can galvanize us into inaction at a time when even the slightest action would prevent tragedy or death. The testimony of the survivors of the tragic crash of two 747 planes on the runway at Tenerife was that hundreds of people simply sat immobile in their seats, not even attempting to escape the flames. Many of those who broke the control of fear managed to escape, while the others stoically awaited their flaming fate.

Fear anesthetizes the mind in such a way as to prevent sound reasoning. Fear keeps us from moving into new areas of life and often causes us to withdraw from even the familiar. Fear can provoke irrational behavior in the best of us, but those whose mental capacities are limited are often greater victims of fear than the rest of us and are less able to rationalize themselves out of its grip.

Fear plagued Grandma Roberts day and night. Mrs. Roberts, well into her seventies, was the oldest member of the Hebron Home family and was affectionately called "Grandma" by the other residents. Although her IQ was sufficiently low to have classified her as retarded, her major problem was one of emotional disorder. She suffered severe depression and extreme anxiety. She was afraid to ride in the bus, lest she be involved in an accident. She was afraid to go for a walk, terrorized that she might get lost. She refused foods unless they were of her choosing, fearing possible poisoning. Her fear of water caused us no small amount of discomfort, as she had to be made to bathe herself or had to be given baths.

Grandma harbored many guilty feelings about her past life. She had given birth to six children but had not bothered to get married. She had lost touch with the children when they were taken from her to be raised in foster homes. As she meditated on this part of her past life, she wrestled with guilt.

Most of the day Grandma read newspapers, or at least held them in front of her with a lost, faraway, detached look on her face. Many times we reassured her that Jesus loved her and that we loved her too. We told her Jesus died so that we might live, and that we need not carry guilt for past actions, but we can have peace in our hearts if we will allow God to forgive our sins and take our guilt away.

At times Grandma would seem to comprehend these statements, but at other times it seemed as though I was talking to the newspaper she sometimes held upside down in front of her.

Then something happened. We were having morning devotions when she seemed to genuinely become aware of what was being said. Mary Harris, one of the counselors, was speaking. "Jesus forgives and loves us," she said, "and He is the creator and ruler of the whole world, so if He forgives and loves us, why don't we forgive and love each other? This is what God wants us to do."

At this point everyone in the home went around the room asking one another's forgiveness—everyone, that is, except Grandma Roberts. She didn't respond in any manner until the others had left for their jobs or school. She had, of course, acknowledged each resident's request for forgiveness with a polite "I forgive you," but she had not moved from her chair.

Getting Mary's attention with a wave of her hand, Grandma said, "If I can forgive others, then why don't I forgive myself? You said God forgives me and you forgive me, so why don't I forgive myself?"

Knowing that Grandma was close to a "breakthrough" in her life, Mary walked over and sat by her and read several passages of Scripture from God's love letter to us, the Bible. As Mary turned to the concordance in the back of her Bible, seeking further passages on forgiveness, she looked into Grandma's face to see if what had already been read had registered. What she saw assured her that further portions of Scripture were not necessary. God's Word had done its wonderful work. Tears flowed over wrinkled, bleached cheeks and fell on weary hands, as a low sob from the depths of this aging woman came struggling to the surface like an air bubble forcing its way to the surface of a pool of strangling mud.

"See, honey, it's easy once you turn it over to the One who knows you best," Mary concluded.

I have seen many emotionally disturbed persons make "breakthroughs" before, but none moved me more than this gentle, fearful old lady when she finally realized she too could experience the peace and joy that so many others in the family had experienced. The change was sudden, to be sure, but there were many old thought patterns and habits to be broken.

That evening Grandma surprised everyone when she came to the table wearing a clean dress and a broad smile. Her hair had been fixed and she smelled like roses. It was too much perfume, perhaps, but what a delightful difference.

Grandma has moved to a home for the aged now. She is happy with her new surroundings and looks forward to the nightly socials. The fearful, withdrawn way of life was replaced with an outgoing, expressive nature that enjoys life. This happened when her guilts were removed.

In neither of these cases did the removal of guilt change the retardation, but it did bring the individuals back to a more normal emotional pattern that enabled them to enjoy life to its fullest.

Retardation is a serious handicap, but it is not the end of life. People have learned to live with extreme physical handicaps and have well-rounded, fulfilled lives. With proper care and training, people with mental handicaps can also learn to live within the range of their abilities and enjoy well-rounded, fulfilled lives. Christians everywhere could contribute to this goal by merely counting the M.R. "in" instead of "out."

6

To Keep or Not to Keep—
That Is the Question

Just as the rain falls upon the tilled and the untilled fields alike, and the sun shines on both the godly and the ungodly, so retarded babies are born to the wealthy and the poor, the educated and the unlearned. Retarded children are found in every level of society and in every race, color, and creed.

It is little comfort to declare that only twenty-three out of each thousand children born are mentally retarded when we realize that this amounts to more than one hundred thousand per year. Actually, a retarded baby is born every five minutes in America, and this means that every five minutes around the clock some family is beginning to face the problem of having to cope with retardation.

For many of these families the doctor's announcement, "We've discovered physical problems pointing to mental retardation," is a serious emotional shock as well as an anticlimax to months of expectation, planning, and dreams. The father had already pictured his son as an outstanding athlete or political figure, or perhaps had planned to add "and son" to the sign on his place of business, while the mother had dreamed of a darling little girl who would someday walk down the aisle in marriage and eventually give birth to a child of her own.

But harsh reality punctures these balloons of ambition at least once every five minutes. "My child is retarded; what are we going to do?" is the nightmare that replaces the beautiful dreams of the past few months.

One of the first problems will be the onset of guilt feelings. There is usually a sense of failure. The fact that the couple may have already given birth to one or more healthy children does not seem to lessen the weight of guilt, for while they will not accept credit for the healthy, natural birth, they readily accept the blame for the deficient one.

Sometimes parents will invest a great amount of time and spend vast sums of money to try to determine the cause of the child's retardation, as though finding the cause would release them from their feelings of personal responsibility. Even if the cause can be pinpointed—and it rarely can—the facts remain the same. Someone very different has been born into the family.

How the parents view this "different" one will

greatly influence their patterns of behavior. If they see this retarded child as an evidence of some failure on their part, or, even worse, as a punishment from God (and, sadly enough, some people's concepts of God encourage this view), their behavior will likely be introverted and negative. If the parents focus their attention on the long-range responsibilities that face them, they may subconsciously withdraw their love from the retarded child, or may transfer that love and attention to another child. It is important that during the early weeks of initial adjustment the husband and wife be honest with each other about their personal feelings, for this will release tension and soften emotional stress.

If, however, the couple can bring themselves to view this "different" one as a "special child," they may very well discover that their awareness for love has been sharpened and quickened. The capacity to receive and respond to the love that most retarded children possess has revitalized the flow of love in more than one home. It seems that in all of nature when one faculty does not function, the other senses sharpen themselves to compensate for the loss. In the retarded, the faculty that develops to compensate for mental slowness or loss is the capacity to love.

Several years ago I saw a poem in a newspaper which so impressed me that I clipped it for my files and have shared it with parents who are facing the initial trauma of adjusting to a mentally retarded baby. It is titled, "Heaven's Very Special Child" and was written by Edna Massimilla. I would like to share it with you.

Heaven's Very Special Child

A meeting was held quite far from earth:
"It's time again for another birth,"
Said the angels to the Lord above.
"This special child will need much love.

"His progress may be very slow;
Accomplishments he may not show,
And he'll require extra care
From the folks he'll meet down there.
He may not run or laugh or play;
His thoughts may seem quite far away.

"In many ways he won't adapt,
And he'll be known as handicapped;
So let's be careful where he's sent—
We want his life to be content.

"Please, Lord, find the parents who
Will do a special job for You.
They will not realize right away
The leading role they're asked to play;
But with this child sent from above
Comes the stronger faith and richer love;

"And soon they'll know the privilege given
In caring for their gift from heaven;
Their precious charge, so meek and mild,
Is Heaven's very special child."

Since obviously there can be no true perspective of any situation when one is self-centered or guilt-ridden, parents of a special child should take time and opportunity for personal growth, using their problem as a stimulant and not as a depressant. The retarded child in the home can be a perplexing problem or an ongoing opportunity. The way it is accepted and handled determines the difference.

Unless there is accompanying physical impairment and severe handicap, the early months of babyhood are not too different from those of other babies. The joy of a new life in the home can be shared and enjoyed by the whole family. The knowledge that development may be impaired in the future need not dull the enjoyment of the baby in the present. If there is any one thing the parents of a special child tend to learn that other parents may miss, it is to grasp each day as an entity in itself and to enjoy whatever possible. Life is not lived in mere future hopes but in present happenings. Instead of looking forward to big things, they learn to enjoy the little things of the "here and now."

But sooner or later the parents of a retarded

child must make a decision about how their child can best be cared for and what is best for the home itself. Basically, there are three options to be considered: to raise the child at home; to put the child in an institution; or to place the child in a foster home or a group training facility. There is something to be said for each option.

Everyone will have advice on the subject, but very often the poorest advice comes from family members. Since it is the parents who must come up with the final decision, it is wise for them to talk with other parents of retarded children. There are also a variety of agencies and organizations for the retarded, both county and state, who could offer experienced counsel. The local telephone directory will help to locate them.

Raising the M.R. at Home

It is my personal opinion, based on my time of working with the retarded, that unless the child is severely retarded, his first six or seven years should be spent at home, for social skills are best learned in the home environment. After this it is often best to put the child in an institution or foster home. But, of course, this is only one option. There are many factors to be considered in making this decision.

For one, the strength of the family "core" needs to be considered. If there are already problems in the home, bringing a retarded child into the situation certainly would not enhance it.

Conversely, it could very well be the proverbial straw that broke the camel's back, for a retarded child demands at least twice as much attention as a normal child. This cannot help affecting the other children in the home and has often been the source of friction between husband and wife.

Furthermore, since the retarded child often has problems with sucking and feeding and is frequently slower at learning toilet training, walking, and talking, his care will be almost as exhausting to the mother as that of a set of twins. In addition to this, very often the "special child" will have other medical problems, and most surely is prone to more childhood diseases and complications.

Assuming sufficient emotional, spiritual, physical and family strength to cope, the decision to raise the retarded child at home may be a profitable one in terms of learning to love and in enjoying unrestrained love from the "special" one. In helping those who are reaching toward this decision, physicians can give advice as to what can be expected in the physical development of the child. Some M.R. children have problems with seizures, motor development, and personality defects which may be released in temper tantrums, prolonged crying or extreme jealousies.

Even more important than learning what lies ahead in the area of physical development is finding out what to expect in the behavior of the retarded child. Here again, a good resource for this information is your local association for the retarded.

I have seen far too many parents raise their "special child" at home, thinking that because their baby was retarded he would always be a child, and consequently always treat him as a small child. This is one of the leading causes of arrested development of M.R. persons. Unless a person is allowed and encouraged to think for himself, and unless he can make decisions on his own at times, he cannot grow mentally, whether he is retarded or normal. To be born mentally retarded is enough of a handicap, but to suffer arrested development of what mental capabilities do exist is tragic.

In September, 1977, *The Alliance Witness* ran an article by Jim Reese, of Ontario, Canada, entitled, "God Can Do Something Wonderful." In this article Mr. Reese told of some of his frustrations at being informed seven hours after the birth of his son that the baby evidenced mental retardation. He and his wife opted to care for the child in their own home, and he gave personal witness to some of the blessings the boy has brought to the family. He concluded his article by listing five things he reviewed regularly. He wrote, "As a parent of a retarded child, there are certain things I must remind myself of from time to time:

"1. I must always thank God for my retarded child. I must never question the goodness of God's intent in giving him to me.

"2. I must view my retarded child not just in the perspective of the now, but in the light of eternity. I must see him as a potentially whole and perfect person in Christ, and I must bend every effort to prepare him for a glorious eternity of fulfillment with Christ.

"3. I must seek, with God's help, to give my retarded child all the educational, physical, social and spiritual advantages that are within my grasp to give.

"4. I must be sensitive to the needs of my normal children by being careful not to short-change them while serving the needs of my handicapped child.

"5. I must nurture the fellowship of others who share a similar concern and build bridges of communication and care to those who have not yet discovered the blessedness of the divine will as it relates to their dilemma."[7]

With principles such as these in operation, a parent might well consider keeping his "special child" in the womb of the home.

But there are still other considerations in deciding what to do about the future of an M.R. child. Not the least of these is the financial concern, for because of the behavior and physical problems, a retarded child costs about twice as much to raise as a normal child. The more severe the retardation, the greater will be the expense. This may well prove to be too great a burden for some families.

Raising the M.R. in an Institution

If the family unit is fragile or the finances are limited, a family may wish to consider a private institution or a state-supported hospital. Although most private institutions are very expensive, there are some that are sponsored by church organizations which may prove to be practical for the modest-income family. Since most private institutions cost $1,000 or more per month, it would be well to check with one's pastor, priest, or rabbi to see if a facility is available in his area that is sponsored by a religious organization. State institutions generally negotiate a fee based on the family income.

Apart from financial considerations, there are still other things involved when exploring the possibility of institutionalizing an M.R. child. Although there are limits to a child's capabilities, depending on the severity of his condition, we have found in recent years, as a result of national interest in the "special child," that the abilities of a retarded person have for the most part been greatly underestimated. Through the use of new methods of training it is possible for retarded persons to learn and understand far more than had been thought possible before.

Many institutions and hospitals employ specialists in skill training. Sometimes teams of workers who have gained much experience with retarded persons can undertake and accomplish goals beyond the abilities of the parents at home.

Another alternative that is gaining popularity throughout the United States is foster home or group training facility placement. The foster home may take one to six children, while the training facility may have six or more "special children" at any given time. Recent licensing requirements in most states insure that these homes are not only safe but that they have regular training periods for their residents.

Usually these homes establish their rates by the degree of care and attention they will have to give the child. Fees are quite varied and range from $100 to $1,000 per month.

Many people have prejudiced opinions regarding institutions for the retarded. It is true that in past years some institutions showed little respect or regard for the handicapped and offered little or no training, but today it is quite different. I have never visited an institution where the retarded individual was not treated with respect and in many places with loving care.

One of the questions regularly asked of me by parents facing the decision of "to keep or not to keep" is, "Won't my child miss me?"

In most cases this is a self-centered question, and what the parent is really asking is, "Can I get along without my child?"

Realistically, most retarded children adapt to a new environment far more quickly than other children do. As they grow older they realize they are different and that they are living at their "school." Usually they take great pride in their surroundings, and a parent should not allow himself to pity his child. Here at Hebron Foundation, we encourage parents to visit their children who are placed in an institution as often as possible. Once a week is not too often. Many places encourage the parent to "work" with the child on his current educational project or therapy class. This encourages the child and the staff and lets them know that the parent still cares.

Because of guilts, imaginary or real, or perhaps because of pity or embarrassment, there are some parents who would rather believe the adage "Out of sight, out of mind."

When I first became the director of Hebron Home I set myself to locate the parents of our residents, for some of them didn't know if their parents were alive or dead, since they had heard nothing from them in over twenty years. I succeeded in locating some of them but found them totally unwilling to make any kind of contact with their children. They had put them out of their minds and lives when they assigned them to an institution, and didn't want old wounds reopened.

Now I spend my energies in urging those parents who are just now entrusting their "special children" to the loving training and supervisory care of an institution, whether it be a large facility, a training center, or a foster home, to keep involved with their children. I encourage them to consider the institution as a boarding school through which they can offer their child specialized care and skills that they may be unable to provide at home. But this does not negate the need for parental love and approval, nor need it separate the child from deeply loving the mother and father.

As I have said, the decision "to keep or not to keep" is entirely the parents' prerogative, but it should not be made on the basis of emotional feelings. There is too much involved to be ruled entirely by deep-seated feelings. An overriding guideline should be what is best for the child. Where can he learn the most? Where will he be the most fulfilled? Should he be forced to compete with normal children and repeatedly fail, or should he be among his peers where he can have a measure of success? Where will he be surrounded by God's love in the most meaningful way?

There is no one right answer, for there are too many variables, but the Christian will seek guidance from God and comfort and understanding from other parents who have been forced to make this decision. Letting the children out of the nest is never easy for the parents, but in the case of the normal child it is the child who basically makes the decision to leave. Schooling progresses to the collegiate level and he has to leave home, or marriage demands that he set up his own household. With the retarded child it is a very different situation. The parent must decide if the child is to leave the nest, and if so, where he will go, and when. It is hard to equate an institution for the retarded with college or a career that moves a child to another community.

It is to be expected that the decision will be painful one, and one that will be deliberated for many months, but it helps lessen the pain when we remind ourselves it is only a decision "to keep or not to keep," not a decision to love or not to love, or to care or not to care. Sometimes love clings, while other times love releases, but true love never stops flowing to its object.

7

"Hear What I Mean"

Are any of us exempt from saying things we do not mean or saying things backwards or awkwardly? Sometimes we playfully call this "foot-in-mouth disease." Because the M.R.'s mind generally works more slowly than the normal person's, and because he often has a limited vocabulary, he seems to suffer from this problem a lot more frequently than do normal persons.

Sometimes this takes on comic proportions as the M.R.s say what they think they have heard, but it comes out very differently. I have had to hide my face behind the hymn book on numerous occasions during the morning devotions, which is a time of prayer, singing and Scripture reading prior to the departure of the residents to their work or schooling. It is a relaxed, enjoyable time for everyone, but sometimes the words to the hymns get slightly mixed up. For instance, "Just as I am, without one plea" has been heard to ring throughout the house as "Just as I am, without one flea," and "Jesus, Savior, pilot me" has come out as "Jesus, Savior, pie and me." I've also chuckled to hear the gospel song; "When the Roll Is Called Up Yonder" come out as "When the roll is cold up yonder I'll be there," and have wondered what the author would have thought if he could have heard his beloved "Old Rugged Cross" sung, "I will cherries the old rugged cross 'til I trophy at last and lie down."

The words didn't quite come out right, but the devotion and sincerity were there. When asked what part of the day he enjoyed the most, one of the residents replied, "I like the morning commotions the best." So be it!

I have had to learn that sometimes the M.R. will speak in reverse; that is, he will use a negative when he means a positive. Last July I encouraged all of the residents of Hebron Home to attend a church summer camp that was situated in the majestic pines between two picturesque rivers. Everyone needs a vacation from the routine tasks of life, and this includes M.R.s. This seemed to me to be a nearly perfect place and time for the "family" to go somewhere together. They would be supportive of each other, and they could compete with one another in ball games, swimming, and archery, as well as enjoy picnics and hiking.

I was, quite frankly, surprised when my

enthusiasm for this trip was not shared by the others. There were all kinds of excuses offered, from "I can't swim" to "I think I will get sick," etc. No one, it seemed, really wanted to go.

After much open discussion at a weekly house meeting, all but three of the residents had agreed it would be fun to go camping. The three hold-outs gave their reasons: "I can't sleep unless I am in my own bed"; "I get sunburned too easily"; and "I want to stay home and catch up on my lessons." (That last excuse gave me a chuckle, for sure.)

Even during the final week of preparations, these three maintained that they wanted to stay home. I didn't want to force them, but I didn't believe they sincerely did not want to go, so two days before departure I announced that the home would be closed during this camping week to enable us to do some renovations. I insisted that anyone staying home would end up working long hours in cleaning and painting.

That night when a final count for campers was called for, everyone enthusiastically raised his hand, including the three hold-outs.

It was a delightful week for the campers, and upon their return home one of the original dissidents enthusiastically reported what a wonderful time he had experienced at the camp and that he was already looking forward to next year's camp.

When I reminded him that for three weeks he

had declared he didn't want to go, he said, "Sometimes I don't mean what I say and sometimes I don't say what I mean. You know what I mean?"

I knew what he meant, and it reminded me of Paul's words in Romans 7:15: "My own behaviour baffles me. For I find myself doing what I really loathe but not doing what I really want to do" (Phillips). My M.R. friend wasn't the first person to have inner conflicts that produced reverse action.

When I am working with retarded persons I have found it imperative to understand the meaning of a statement rather than to rely too heavily on the word-for-word definition of that statement. After all, words are only tools by which we seek to convey our thoughts and feelings. We should seek to catch particular thoughts or emotions rather than to get lost in the semantics of its expression.

I try to tune myself into the thought frequencies of the mentally retarded by putting myself "inside" of them, attempting to think as they think and feel what they feel. Happily, the slowdown of their minds does not numb their sense of feeling or hinder their longings to love and be loved. Often when I try placing myself in their circumstances it gives me fresh insights into what they are really trying to express. Maybe it is recognition that they want, or love, or acceptance. Perhaps they are experiencing cravings that come with our physical nature, but they have never been shown how to express or satisfy those cravings.

This was Crissy's problem. No one had understood what was going on inside her. She was a very attractive young lady about twenty-five years of age. Her golden blonde hair cascaded to her shoulders, and her fair, unblemished complexion attested that she was a natural blonde. In addition to this, she had a trim, well-proportioned figure.

Crissy had spent several years in various state institutions because her family could not cope with her promiscuous activities. Somehow they could not control her, and she was a great source of embarrassment to all who knew her or had responsibility for her.

Crissy functioned on the level of an eleven-year-old and was quite conversant. I was amazed that she showed no signs of guilt for her actions, although the severity of the situation had been explained to her several times.

Even after several counseling sessions with her I was still at a loss as to what caused her self-destructive actions. I explored the possibilities that she might need a "father image" in her life; that perhaps she had had an overly protective family environment; and everything else I could think of that might unlock the cause of her promiscuity. But nothing worked. I was up against a blank wall.

One afternoon while I was again explaining to her what our responsibilities in life are, especially in the areas of love and sex, she began crying and slowly sobbed out, "But I am a woman, and I want to have a baby."

I wasn't prepared for that, and I had to pretend to get something from the filing cabinet to keep her from seeing how startled I actually was.

As I regained my composure I realized that for the first time I had a true point of contact with her problem of misdirected sexuality. She was experiencing a normal longing for a baby, so I responded by explaining to her that there was a proper time for all things, and that families followed marriage—they did not precede it.

"But I want a baby now," she interrupted. "I want a baby so I can take care of it, feed it, clean it, and love it."

"Okay, Crissy," I said. "Let's pray about it right now. I think God is interested in your desire."

Joining hands with her, I led her in a prayer of open confession to God that she deeply desired to have a baby all her own. She enthusiastically said the "amen" at the close of the prayer, and then just stared into my eyes, alive with expectation.

"I'm sure God understands your feelings," I finally said, "and I think I am beginning to know what you deeply desire. I think you should have a baby, too."

The surprise on her face matched the shock in my heart, for neither of us really expected me to say that.

"A baby will be a great responsibility for you," I continued. "You will have to take care of it all the time, and with your schoolwork and household chores it certainly won't leave you very much time for yourself."

"I don't care about that," she said. "I just want to have a baby to love and train so I can watch it grow up."

I told her we would talk about it more the next day.

To say she had the entire home upset by telling everyone she was going to have a baby would be the understatement of the year.

The next morning she ran to meet me before I could even get out of my Mazda.

"Did you really mean what you said yesterday?" she challenged me. "Are you going to let me have a baby?"

"Crissy," I said, "today you will be a mother," and I opened the box on the front seat of the car. Lifting out a fluffy white poddle puppy, I handed it to her ever so gently.

"Lots of people have human babies," I said, "but not very many people are lucky enough to have a poodle to take care of and to love. He is yours. He's your baby now."

Tears flowed freely as she lifted the bundle of fur to her face. My fear that she would be disappointed dissolved as I saw the sparkle in her tear-drenched eyes. Reaching tall on her tiptoes, she planted a kiss on my cheek and said, ever so lovingly, "God is good to me."

I knew God was indeed good, not only to Crissy, but to me also in helping me find that key to unlock her problem.

Crissy returned to her family and is a devoted "mother" who is no longer promiscuous. Faithful to her promise to me, she is also working toward getting her high school diploma.

Crissy merely needed someone to really hear what she was saying. Don't we all?

8

"Recognize What I Can Do!"

When dealing with the educable M.R. person, where an acceptable level of communication exists, it is relatively easy to effect a change. But when we are confronted with the severely and profoundly retarded, it is an entirely different situation. Many of these have not developed a verbal communication channel beyond a few single words, and they rely on grunts, gestures, and pointing.

Since these levels of retardation comprise such a small percentage of all M.R.s (less than 5 percent), and because they do not generally respond to counseling and training, they are often institutionalized. Beyond basic physical care, they are left alone, abandoned to their limited and often confused mental world.

While Hebron Home is not equipped and staffed to provide care for these profoundly retarded individuals, I have often observed them on my regular visits to the state institutions that do care for them. I have looked into their lifeless eyes and blank faces and have wondered what was going on inside of them.

"Is it possible," I have wondered, "that the breakdown is more in their ability to express than in their capacity to comprehend? Could their spirits be aware even if their minds (a capacity of the soul) are basically unproductive?"

Present research does not have answers to my questions, but some of us who are devoting our lives to caring for the mentally retarded have had some experiences and have made some observations which lead me to believe that most of the retarded, regardless of their IQ level, can be helped to make a step, however small, toward normalization. I am not suggesting that they can be moved from the profound classification, for this usually is the result of severe physical impairment. What I do feel, nonetheless, is that their behavioral characteristics can be altered toward normalcy in at least some areas of their lives.

The authors of the book, *Occupational Therapy for Mentally Retarded Children*, state, "Unlike the intellectual, perceptual, and physical differences of a retarded child that are directly related to the amount of retardation, behavioral characteristics are not necessarily a result of the retardation. Behavioral problems or expressions of conflict reflect an imbalance between the child's abilities and the requirements of the environment.

"Since these behavioral characteristics are often a result of the attitudes and methods with which normal persons deal with the retarded child, these characteristics can often be modified as a result of a change in the expectations of those dealing with the child."[8]

"Is it not likely," I reasoned, "that some, if not much, of the behavior characteristics of the severely retarded are fundamentally a response to the treatment they received? Since almost nothing was expected of them, their responses were blank."

All of us need challenges and goals, but they cannot be beyond our ability to achieve them or they will produce frustration rather than fulfillment. If this is true of the normal person, how much more true it must be for the subnormal person— even the sub-subnormal.

"But how can I challenge a person who is so severely handicapped mentally that he doesn't even communicate verbally?" I asked myself. "How would I ever be able to set goals for such a person?"

I got my first good clue in dealing with Tracy.

While working with the staff in a state hospital in Oregon, I was asked if I would observe and perhaps attempt to communicate with and counsel Tracy. He was a young man about thirty years old who was afflicted with Down's syndrome, which used to be called "Mongolism." It seemed like a hopeless assignment, for he had no verbal communication at all; he relied on a series of grunting sounds to gain attention or to show his approval or disapproval. Furthermore, the staff at the hospital had failed to communicate with him effectively, so I wondered how I could succeed where they had failed.

Because of the severity of the problem Tracy was causing the staff, I finally agreed to study him, seeking some clue that might help me reach him and adjust his behavior to at least a tolerable level.

Tracy's problem, to state it rather bluntly, was that he was a "feces draw-er." He would remove his stools from the toilet and smear them on the wall of the bathroom.

After observing his bizarre actions for a period of time, I began to notice that there was a definite pattern in his smearings. Because I am a practiced painter, I thought I saw an "art form" in his actions, so I urged the staff to hang butcher paper on the wall nearest the toilet and to fix a tray of finger paints directly under it.

Almost immediately Tracy transferred his painting mediums. With the improved vehicles it wasn't very long until the entire staff could see true art forms emerging, so they encouraged him to use these finger paints as many times a day as he desired and for as long a period as he desired.

Slowly the staff transferred his "studio" from the rest room to the lounge area, and I began to introduce him to the use of brushes and water colors. As his expertise improved I showed him how to use charcoal to express artistically what was inside him. Within three weeks his problem in the bathroom was solved, and he was drawing pictures of recognizable objects, even combining different scenes with color and shadows. From memory he would paint scenes he had viewed from the hospital windows. Through his artistic talent he was letting us know some of the things that were going on in his mind. He was observing and relating to much more of his surroundings than we had dared to believe possible.

Although Tracy can never hope to obtain gainful employment in the "outside world," this newly discovered talent gave him a useful world right in the hospital. What began as an artificial or therapeutic interest in his work turned to genuine appreciation, and first the staff and then "outsiders" began to purchase his work. He is by no means self-supporting, but he does earn enough money through the sale of his artwork to purchase his clothes, supplies, and treats.

I did not train him to be an artist; I merely recognized his artistic talent. I was able to see beyond the filthy mess he created daily and discern a desperate cry to express whatever part of his mind had developed. By understanding his need for attention and expression, we were able to help him achieve some semblance of normalization.

Thankfully, not all cases are so complicated as

Tracy's, but his situation and its solution do underline the need to establish a line of communication with the mentally retarded person no matter what level of severity he may be in. He, like us, has needs that cry for fulfillment, no matter how limited his capacity may be. By directing these needs into positive channels of expression we may be able to help him to realize and fulfill his dreams; and, after all, isn't that what life is all about?

The infant can completely fulfill himself with a rattle or teething ring, while a two-year-old would prefer a sand pile, bucket and shovel. Each finds expression and complete fulfillment, and none of us laments their inability to appreciate a symphony or drive a car. As long as they are reaching their maximum level of achievement, both they and we are satisfied.

But the teen-ager who is restricted to the sandbox as his total fulfillment in life will rebel, for as life develops it seeks higher goals and greater levels of expression and fulfillment.

It is no different with the mentally retarded, except that they move at a much slower pace. But they do move, and to confine them to the sandbox builds the same frustrations in them that it would build in us.

Sometimes the greatest function of love is merely recognizing development in others and encouraging and teaching them how to relate to and fulfill themselves at this new level. Perhaps this is the challenge that keeps me working with the mentally retarded. I keep wondering how many more Tracys there are who are being disciplined for rebellion when all they are saying is, "I don't get fulfillment with a rattle any more; can't I play in the sandbox for a while?"

In Tracy's case it took an artist to recognize an artist. But since we've all progressed through the various stages of maturity, shouldn't we be able to recognize where they are coming from? All it takes is a little observation, a jogging of our memory, and a willingness to identify with whatever intellectual and emotional level we may discover in the M.R. It can mean the difference between fulfillment and frustration for the M.R. if we will recognize their abilities, however limited they may be, rather than dramatize their inabilities.

9

Loved to Death

"What the M.R. needs most is lots of love," the articles in the popular press often say.

"I don't know if your training facility can show my child the amount of love he has become accustomed to," parents often tell our admissions director.

"I give my M.R. child more love than I give to all the rest of my family put together, and yet he becomes more incorrigible every month," a distraught mother says in the counseling room.

Is love really the answer to the M.R.'s problem? Yes, it is; if by love we mean concern for their best interests and a willingness to sacrifice and become involved to see that they receive the finest care and opportunities to grow, expand, and develop which are within our reach.

Characteristically, though, this is not always what is meant by "love." I have seen too many M.R.s who have been seriously prevented from developing in areas where they had the capacity to mature simply because a smothering love replaced a mother love. Everything was done for "the little darling." Because the M.R. child is unable to keep up with his peers in the development of a particular skill, some parents assume that the M.R. will never develop skill in that area. Therefore, during the years when the retarded one remained at home, particular developmental skills he could master were done for him.

Some parents overprotect their M.R. child by refusing to expose him to normal children. The child is a forced recluse who becomes socially retarded in addition to his other handicaps. It may seem like love to insulate the retarded one from any potential mockery or from competition with far more competent children, but at the same time it limits his chance to make improvements, adjustments, and adaptations to the "outside world."

Many a mother has stood at her window weeping as she watched her retarded child attempting to compete with the other children in the neighborhood. Everything in her emotional nature wants to rush out and rescue him from the repeated humiliation his failures have brought him, but her true mother's heart overrules her emotions, for she realizes that if she shelters him from everything he will never become self-sufficient in any way. Her true love bears the hurts to enable the child to experience enlargement.

Does a retarded child need more love than a normal child? How can a parent measure his love for the children in the family? Five children in a household are not given one-fifth of each parent's love; each is given all of it. No, the retarded do not need more love, but they may need to be reassured of that love far more frequently than the others in the home. They will need to have that love demonstrated far more often in time-consuming care and provision for personal needs.

A parent will have the same measure of love for the infant as he has for his teen-aged child, but it will be manifested quite differently through the various stages of that child's development. True love will stop doing whenever the child shows the ability to do for himself, and that ability comes through loving training. No teen-ager wants to be smothered with the expression of love that delights a baby. Neither does a maturing M.R.

How often we have taken into our training facility M.R.s who were dressed as little boys or girls and who were treated accordingly by their parents. Yet when we asked the age of the M.R., the parents admitted that their child was over thirty years of age. Our training later proved they acted like six-year-olds because they had always been treated like six-year-olds. When we showed sufficient love to let them mature into whatever level of adulthood they could manage to attain, the change was dramatic. The parents called it a miracle; we merely called it a release. We simply stopped smothering them and allowed them to develop socially. We most certainly did not love them more than the parents had loved them over those many years, but we loved them differently. We did not smother them with loving attention, we loved them enough to pull back and let them experience life. Of course we instructed them, encouraged and motivated them, and we were always there to pick them up after a failure, but we convinced them that we loved them enough to help them learn to live on their own as much as possible.

Sometimes the effects of this overprotective, smothering love remain in the M.R.s for many years. Some build up deep resentments and even hatred toward their parents when they discover how far they are able to develop after being released from that suppressing love. We have had to teach many of them to forgive their parents and have been agents of reconciliation for many of them.

Such controlling, forceful love sometimes produces effects which erupt in strange ways. Ronnie illustrates this quite vividly. The doctors declared that he was mentally retarded with incipient schizophrenic tendencies of the residual type, but there was a time when you would hardly have known that Ronnie was any different from the other boys in his parochial school classes. Although he was always a slow learner, he had managed to maintain a grade point average that enabled him to pass from grade to grade until he entered high school. Unable to equal the scholastic and athletic achievements of his three older brothers who were excellent students and gifted athletes, Ronnie's defense was to retire into the safe, quiet world of his own mind and live unto himself.

His mother's response to this was to do everything for him. She became a protective mother hen, constantly coddling Ronnie under her wings. Ronnie succumbed to this, quit school, and pretty well dropped out of the world of reality. Mother would protect him, provide for him, and do for him, so he just vegetated. But then mother was cut out of his life and he couldn't cope with the loss. By the time we met Ronnie he had been in several facilities for the retarded and in one institution for the mentally ill.

Ronnie has now lived at Hebron Home for four years. He is a tall, lean, muscular man in his mid-thirties who is usually an easygoing person, and although he stays pretty much to himself he is a very willing worker. It pleased us to see such a spark of enthusiasm when we assigned him the task of caring for a hutch of rabbits behind the garage at Hebron Home. Very quickly Ronnie assigned names to the rabbits and began to treat them like lifetime friends. He could frequently be heard holding conversations with them, supplying both sides of the conversation. He laughed and joked with them regularly.

Although his behavior violated our policy of "enforcing normal behavior in place of abnormal action," we felt that this activity was good for Ronnie because talking to his friends, the rabbits, had somehow opened him to communicate with his peers in the home. We felt the benefits warranted a relaxing of the rules, for, after all, results are what the rules are all about. Ronnie loved to tell the other residents about his rabbits, always being very specific about which rabbit was being discussed.

When we discovered a large doe rabbit making a nest in the cage, we explained to Ronnie that she was about to become a mother and that he would soon have some baby rabbits to care for. His excitement almost rivaled that of an expectant father. It was the only thing he would talk about for days.

When the litter came, Ronnie would not allow anyone other than himself to care for them, almost as though they were sacred and he was their priest. He certainly was the ideal "father" and often acted as a substitute mother as well.

One evening I was aware that the shower seemed to be running endlessly. As I looked around the front room and dining area, it seemed that all were present—or were they? Where was Ronnie? Certainly he wouldn't be showering this late in the evening, and anyway, he never stayed in the shower this long.

Like a parent who becomes suspicious when the children are silent, I started to wonder, so I slipped to Ronnie's room to check things out. The blood-soaked clothes lying on the foot of his bed confirmed my suspicions. Something had gone wrong.

Stepping into the bathroom, I called him out of the shower stall and asked him, "Would you like to tell me what has happened, Ronnie?" as I displayed his blood-soaked trousers.

Without saying a word, he dressed and then motioned for me to follow him outside. Although we do not have lights behind the garage, even the pale light of the stars revealed more than I wanted to see. The doors to all the rabbit hutches were swung wide open and there were mounds of white fur on the ground in front of the pens. Whereas a few hours ago there had been sixteen rabbits in those cages, now there were only lifeless, headless corpses strewn around the yard.

Before I could say a word, Ronnie broke into a soft, whimpering sort of cry. "I tried to show them I loved them," he blurted out. "I just patted them lovingly; then I patted them harder and harder. I couldn't stop."

Stooping to pick up a ball of fur from the ground in front of him, he sobbed, "They're no good now. I have ruined them all." With that he silently retreated into the house.

Perhaps a skilled psychologist could explain the reasons for and the ramifications of Ronnie's new and bizarre behavior. Whether or not the diagnosis would say that he was only expressing the kind of love he had received in virtually "loving to death," we at the home certainly saw what happened as a prime example of this. In extending smothering love, Ronnie had destroyed the very thing he cherished the most. So have many rightly motivated but wrongly actuated parents done to their dependent but retarded little ones. Mature love can back up far enough to allow growth.

10

Mable's Graduation Party

Because the M.R. is slow to grasp new concepts and tends to resist any change in his living routine, we often shield him from many of the harsh realities of life's changing patterns. Furthermore, most M.R.s need a fairly stable emotional climate in which to function. Extremes should be avoided as much as possible. It just doesn't seem fair to overload a person who is already operating on only four cylinders.

But there are some harsh realities of life that cannot always be controlled or even modified. Mable's unexpected death was certainly one of these instances.

Mable had been on the sick list for many months, but not for anything very serious. It seemed that she always had something to keep her in her room reading her Bible. For a while it was high blood pressure with accompanying headaches, but the doctor didn't feel that her pressure was significantly high. Other times a chest cold would hang on for weeks, but frequent trips to the doctor's office kept her supplied with cough syrups and antibiotics.

As I said, Mable never had any serious illnesses, but she had a consistent series of physical complaints. She was lovingly viewed as our resident hypochondriac.

Then in mid-February a chest cold that had persisted for many weeks developed into pneumonia, and before anyone on the staff realized what was happening, Mable died.

There was no way to keep it from the residents. Her death caught all of us by surprise. I wondered how the rest of the family would be able to face this grim reality.

My father had been a pastor during my childhood days, and I had watched him try to hold families together during their hours of grief. Quite honestly, I used to wonder at people's professed faith in God and in life after death because of their negative reactions after the death of a loved one.

Of course, I realized that death was traumatic, and the awareness that we will no longer enjoy the company of that loved one here on earth is bound to bring grief to those who are left behind. Still, I used to feel that if people really believed that their Christian loved one was with Christ in heaven, as was so loudly professed in the parsonage and funeral parlor, and that their fears, failures, pains, and labors of this world had been replaced with faith, fulfillment, pleasure, health, and rest, then, I reasoned, should not there be a time of rejoicing at the passing of a Christian friend?

Maturity has a way of replacing the idealism of youth with the cold facts of reality. Few adults face death positively. It is generally viewed as a tragic end to a fruitful life. Grief, sorrow, remorse, self-pity, and even guilt feelings seem to be the overriding emotions displayed.

"If this is the way 'normal' people respond to death—especially unexpected death—what are going to be the reactions of our retarded residents?" I asked a staff member.

Mable's funeral was very simple and unpretentious. No relatives attended. Aside from the minister and a couple of social workers, the only people who came to the graveside services were her "brothers and sisters" from Hebron Home.

As the bus pulled out of the cemetery en route back to Hebron Home, the silence among its passengers was painful. Not a word was spoken.

"Has it been too much of a shock?" I wondered. "Are they bottling up their grief, unable to communicate it? Should I try to initiate a discussion about Mable's death to defuse this emotional time bomb?"

But my concern was unnecessary. They were merely thinking, for after a lengthy silence someone mentioned that Mable wouldn't have to do the dishes any more.

"That's right," another responded. "She won't have to do any work at all from now on. Besides that, she can sleep in every day that she wants to, not just on Saturday mornings."

With that breaking of the ice, the tempo of the conversation picked up, and soon all were rejoicing at Mable's "graduation" into a new home where she would never be sick, where she would be like everyone else, and where all of her needs would be fulfilled.

This sort of discussion continued until the bus pulled up in front of the home. The walk to the house was spirited and almost animated.

In the front room someone suggested that since Mable would not be present for her birthday, maybe we could give her a combination birthday and graduation party. The suggestion was received with enthusiasm in a unanimous and spontaneous voicing of approval.

Relieved that the residents had taken such a positive position toward Mable's death, the staff rushed preparations for the party. Punch was made while a staff member hurried to the local bakery to pick up some cakes and cookies. A few well-used decorations were brought out of the closet and arranged around the table. Sandwiches were made by the ladies of the home, while the fellows gathered the chairs around the elongated table in the dining room. It seemed that everyone was involved. After all, it was two parties in one, wasn't it?

I doubt if we have ever had a more successful party. One by one the residents testified to the goodness Mable had shown to them, while some expressed their anticipation at seeing her when they too "graduated" to heaven. It was truly a testimonial banquet in their eyes.

Later, one of the staff confided in me that the passing of Mable had forcibly reminded her of the loss of her own dear friend a few months earlier. She said that seeing the healthy attitude and positive action of the residents during their personal loss had caused her to feel ashamed of the selfishness she had felt in her own loss.

I, too, benefited from the experience, for I saw the reality of Revelation 21:4: "And God shall wipe away all tears from their eyes" and 1 John 3:2: ". . . we shall be like him, for we shall see him as he is." Here I had virtually put the staff on an "emergency alert," and instead of our ministering to the distraught residents, they innocently taught us a lesson. Death is a part of life that needs to be accepted as naturally as any other major change. These special people proved themselves capable of this adjustment.

Perhaps "graduation parties" should become a part of all Christian funerals.

11

"Please Help Me Communicate With You"

Although Hebron Home is located directly across the street from the public school complex right in the heart of Mt. Angel, Oregon, we utilize the fertile soil of the vacant lot to the north of the house for a small vegetable garden. This not only gives the residents another learning experience but provides fresh vegetables for the table.

Last year, right between the tomatoes and the squash I planted a row of bush beans, even though the Willamette Valley is noted for its production of pole beans. All of our special people at the home were excited to see this "strange" type of bean grow so prolifically.

One evening in mid-August I suggested to the cook that we have some fresh beans with our supper.

"I don't have time to pick them now," she said. "Perhaps tomorrow."

"No problem," I answered. "I'll send the twins out to pick them, and have Margaret come in and prepare them for you."

"Hank, Harry!" I called to the fifty-year-old twin residents. "Rush out into the garden, and each of you pick two big handfuls of the bush beans. Hurry, we want them for supper."

Excited at this special assignment, the men rushed into the garden. Each grabbed a plant at its base right next to the ground and uprooted it completely. Returning to the kitchen with a full bush of beans in each hand, they asked expectantly, "Was this fast enough?"

I had given an order, but I had not really communicated. When I asked for two handfuls of beans I didn't mean the plants, but that was what the twins had understood me to say. I had used words that were clear enough to my mind, but they had painted quite a different picture in the minds of the twins.

When the mind is working at less than full capacity, and when physical handicaps further limit expression, verbal communication suffers. Obviously, the greater the mental and physical impairment is, the greater the limitation of expression.

A paper by R. William English and Jerry L. Harris that was released by the University of Oregon, Eugene, Oregon, in May, 1977, affirms, "The notion that mentally retarded persons are deficient in their ability to understand and effectively use language in critical life situations has gained widespread acceptance in recent years." The paper chronicles the findings of these two men who had conducted a series of interviews with mildly retarded and nonretarded persons. They concluded that even the mildly retarded persons had some difficulty with four of eight language dimensions (abstractness, orientation, accuracy/length, and comprehension). No interviews were conducted with the more severely retarded.

Since 75 to 85 percent of persons labeled M.R. fall into the "mild" range with IQs of between fifty and seventy-five, and these are far more verbal than the other classes of retardation, it affords optimism for using verbal counseling as a treatment tool for retarded persons; but it also flashes the warning sign, "Proceed with caution."

While using my brother Judson's office some time back, I was amused at a small plaque he had on his desk. It read, "I know you believe you understand what you think I said, but I am not sure you realize that what you heard is not what I meant."

"That's the story of my life," I declared. How often have I "clearly" explained a situation to the special persons at Hebron Home and have received a positive response in return; yet later, when the explanation was being implemented, I discovered how differently they understood my communication from the way I understood it. I had talked with them, but we had not really communicated—at least not very accurately.

Of course, this is not merely because they are mentally retarded, for this happens in relating to the nonretarded as well, but the difficulty of accurate communication is always compounded when dealing with any level of retardation.

I have found that Paul's principle, "We then that are strong ought to bear the infirmities of the weak, and not to please ourselves" (Romans 15:1), fits the problem of communicating with the retarded. If they cannot reach my level of expression, I will lower my speech patterns to match their capacity to understand. This is not condescension but adaptation. It is what the father does in establishing rapport with his pre-school children. He restricts his vocabulary to their experience level.

I find I can save much time and be much more effective if I can get some idea of the level of verbal expression of the person with whom I am trying to communicate, for comprehension is greatly increased when I direct my conversation to the level of the retarded person's own verbal skills.

I constantly remind my staff that complex words and concepts often reflect abstraction that is more lofty than most retarded persons can deal with. Words like "affiliation" and "adjustment" are best changed to less complex words like "belonging" and "satisfaction."

I have also discovered that a slightly slower and

more deliberate speech delivery improves communication. This might include closer eye contact and a more forward, open posturing.

In helping the retarded persons learn how to communicate effectively, I earnestly seek not to guess at what they mean; I encourage them to speak their thoughts and feelings more specifically until I am certain that I have understood them.

For instance, assume that I do not understand the retarded person's statement of reality and that I must "discover" it. Close-ended questions won't reveal very much to me, for if I ask, "Do you like your new roommate?" I will probably get a simple "yes" or "no." But if I ask open-ended questions such as, "What is there that you enjoy (or dislike) about your new roommate?" I am far more likely to gain both information and feelings, both of which are important if I am ever going to understand this person's inner thoughts.

These open-ended questions also help me to better determine whether the person is accurately verbalizing his feelings, and whether or not he really understands and means what he says.

Knowing the feelings and the level of honesty in their communication has proved to be very important in my communication with retarded persons, for most of them have long histories of depending on others and are therefore highly suggestible and easily persuaded by others.

In order to habilitate the retarded person and to bring him a step closer to normalcy, we must try to make him function as independently as possible. Every decision made for him only increases his dependency upon others.

Of course, this does not mean that we will quietly stand by while he makes a major decision that will probably result in a failing experience, but it does mean we will communicate our feelings about his decision rather than simply countermanding it.

Most of us communicate our feelings to the mentally retarded without being consciously aware of that communication. Koch reminds us, "Most retarded people are very much aware of the motives of other people. They sense whether or not a person is sincere or just making fun of them. They realize that they are different and have special problems."[9]

I would go even further than that, based on my years of working with all levels of retarded persons, and say that most retarded people are very much aware that other persons find them offensive and undesirable. Movements to restrict the number of facilities for the retarded in any given community only underscore the public attitude toward having them around. Knowing this produces deep feelings, for although they may be designated as mentally retarded, this does not invalidate their capacity to feel; quite to the contrary, they are very often keenly sensitive persons.

When they get repeated signals of rejection,

their feelings are often reflected internally in undesirable ways. A common response is for the retarded person to try to deny his condition, or to succumb to self-pity for being retarded. Rarely do retarded persons accept their disability for what it is.

I have found it absolutely imperative to lovingly help the retarded person to understand his disability and to show him that the feelings projected to him from other people are often little more than an extending of their own personal problems, such as fears, insecurities, or ignorance of mental retardation. Because the nonretarded person does not understand retardation he does not know how to cope with it, and so he often overreacts. Unless the retarded person has some understanding of this, he may accept the blame for the rejection and be driven deeper inward instead of coming outward in expressing himself to others. After all, self-expression requires some degree of acceptance by others.

To help all of us on the staff maintain a constant awareness of this need to be accepted in order to be able to communicate, I typed out ten guidelines which I posted in the office as our "Daily Reminder":

1. I am to encourage the residents to respond normally to everyday activity.

2. A soft voice turns away anger. I will not yell or show anger.

3. I will remember that each resident has his

own particular problem.

4. Although I do not understand all of the reasons for a resident acting the way he does, I will respond with love.

5. I am not in competition with the residents, so I need not try to prove myself to be right.

6. I will always ACT and not REACT.

7. I must remember to listen to others.

8. I will try to explain the reasons for my actions to the residents, not to justify my actions but to help the residents to understand these actions.

9. I will "weigh" my words. Swearing and vulgar language decrease my effectiveness with the residents.

10. I will at all times regard the residents as viable adult human beings, capable of learning and deserving the right to live as normal citizens.

Our goal at Hebron Home is to offer guidance in life situations to the special people who live there. We know from experience that influence is necessary before guidance will be accepted, and love is the strongest influence that can be exerted. But love does not exert an influence until it is accepted. As a matter of fact, love has not truly been communicated until it is received, for there is no communication until there is acceptance. That is why consistent, Christ-like attitudes must be maintained by the staff. This creates a climate where love will be both received and returned, for none but the worst cynics can consistently reject love that is consistently and gently offered.

Love communication is somewhat like the salt in Christ's parable in the Bible. It can bring out the flavor or goodness in people. Salt, by itself, has little flavor of its own, but when properly applied to food it brings out the natural goodness in everything it touches. So does love. Sometimes love brings out unexpected things in others, as it did in the case of Conrad.

Almost any special occasion is accepted as an excuse for a party at Hebron Home, and this party was one of those occasions. The punch was flowing, and sticky fingers and white frosting on smiling faces were a testimony that the cake had been enjoyed.

Conrad, age fifty-seven, was sitting in his favorite chair watching while some of the residents gathered around the piano for a songfest. Other residents had started a Monopoly game in the sun room, but Conrad just sat and watched. Conrad was deaf and mute. His only living relative was a brother who had told us that Conrad had spoken and could hear when he was a child, but since the age of fourteen years he had not spoken a word.

Conrad was a tender man, never a problem; he did his chores and stayed out of people's way. But he lived pretty much to himself.

I walked over to him, sat on the arm of his chair, and slipped an arm around his shoulder. I felt such a compassion for this man that although I knew he could not hear me, I said aloud, "Conrad, if you could have anything in the world right now, what would it be?"

To my utter amazement, without turning his head toward me he said, "More cake."

We both jumped at the sound of his voice. Several of the residents heard him and came running toward us, screaming, "Conrad talked, Conrad talked."

The whole experience was so overwhelming that Conrad started to cry and went to his room.

"More cake" is not much communication, but it was more than he had expressed in forty-three years. It was a start. Love and attention "broke the ice" for Conrad, and the staff has worked hard to keep the ice from refreezing by making him verbally ask for special items. His speech has improved rapidly. I expect there will be further breakthroughs for him in the future.

12

"Is It Hopeless?"

The anxiety, emotional pain, and feelings of futility experienced by parents of M.R.s can be fully understood only by other parents of "special children." The rest of us feel sorry for them but are seldom sufficiently involved to know the depth of despair with which many of these parents wrestle. About the time they resign themselves to accept the limitations of their child, something happens to stir fresh hope that he may be outgrowing it, for often they have survived on hope.

From the moment their baby was diagnosed as "retarded" they have earnestly sought for a cure, even telling themselves that they would be satisfied with even a partial remission. Sometimes they have gone from doctor to doctor and from clinic to clinic, and parents have uprooted the whole family and moved to another community where specialized help was available.

This has often brought criticism from family and friends who from their "outside-looking-in" position feel that the inevitable should be accepted and that living in hope of a future change jeopardizes happiness in the present. They argue that the doctors have decidedly declared that there is no hope; that brain cells cannot be generated, and that retardation cannot be cured. "Live with the facts and stop tantalizing yourself by seeking the unobtainable," they say.

But suppose we had taken that same posture toward polio some years ago. That, too, seemed to be hopeless, but someone kept hope alive until an effective preventive was discovered and implemented.

Again, suppose our scientists' dream of walking on the moon had been put aside as completely unattainable, or that man's hope to fly had actually been abandoned because of the many failures men had experienced in their attempts. It has been said that most major inventions have come through men who did not know that a certain thing could not be done.

Whenever hope dies, man ceases to progress. The Psalmist cried, "Uphold me according unto thy word, that I may live: and let me not be ashamed of my hope" (Psalm 119:116). No parent of an M.R. should be shamed for hoping for a change in his child. There is nothing wrong with hope; as a matter of fact, it is a divine gift of God. Paul wrote, "Now abideth faith, hope, charity, these three" (1 Corinthians 13:13), and even declares that "We thank [God] for you, because we have heard of the *faith* you hold in Christ Jesus, and the *love* you bear towards all God's people. *Both spring from the hope* stored up for you in heaven—that hope of which you learned when the message of the true Gospel first came to you" (Colossians 1:3-5, NEB emphasis added). So hope is the wellspring from which faith and love flow: no hope—no love or faith.

No, there is nothing wrong with abiding in hope, for God has put it in the nature of man to be discontent with the way things are and to refuse the concept that they cannot be changed.

Nonetheless, it is possible to become a prisoner of hope. Even the Scriptures speak of people who are "prisoners of hope" (Zechariah 9:12). If hope has made us passive it is destructive, for nothing changes without the expenditure of great energy. Merely sitting back "hoping" that things will improve is little more than self-deception. Hope is not a prison warden; it is intended to be a goad that prods us into action. Hope should be a driving force that motivates us to superhuman efforts. It should be our guiding light in the dark places, and our crutch or cane when we think we are too weary or fragile to go on.

Hope causes the mind to become not inert, but inspired. It is like the fresh morning breeze that clears away the fog, revealing the beauty of the day. To the parents of an M.R. child, hope is a way of life; without it they merely exist. Let none take away their hope!

Howbeit, when avenue after avenue has proved to be a dead end, and dream after dream turns out to be a nightmare, hope is often worn fragile and is replaced with despair. "It's no use; nothing has helped, and nothing will help," is their desperate lament. Medical science may seem to agree with them, and so do the statistics, but is it possible that the foundation of this sense of hopelessness is having hoped for too much too soon? We all like the miracle cure stories, and dreams seldom stay very close to reality. But true hope will be content with lesser successes while never losing sight of the greater dream. Perhaps it is unrealistic to expect a "cure" for retardation to be found during our lifetime, but what has been discovered that can help the M.R.? What training is available? What opportunities in life can be afforded this "special child"?

In general, there is a realistic hope of his being accepted by society. An awakened awareness in Americans has brought retardation out of the closet into the front room. The shame is being replaced with sharing. More and more special education is being made available to the handicapped, and job opportunities are more plentiful to the retarded than ever before. Special summer camps are scheduled for M.R.s throughout the country, and even theatrical performances are being staged by the retarded.

Although prejudices and misunderstandings still exist in many people's minds, more progress seems to have been made in creating a climate of acceptance during this decade than in previous generations. There is reason to hope that this public understanding will increase, not decrease, in the next ten or so years, and as this becomes a reality the stigma of retardation will be greatly lessened, thereby easing the pain of living in a normal world.

There are many tasks for which the retarded are qualified that others refuse to accept as employment, such as housework, menial labor, assembly line work, and so forth. These jobs can be both challenging and fulfilling to the retarded, but in the past they have often been denied them because of prejudice and lack of understanding of how to fit the retarded into the labor force. This is changing.

Because of this, many of the mildly retarded, who comprise 89 percent of M.R.s, are already integrated into society, living quite fulfilled lives. They work, marry, and bear children (who, by the way, are usually normal).

The moderately retarded, who comprise 6 percent of all M.R.s, are capable of learning functional academic skills; they can be quite independent in familiar surroundings, and in sheltered conditions can perform semi-skilled work. No longer must they be "mother's little boy" until their dying day; with proper training they can become mature men and women. They are much slower to learn and acquire skills than their normal brothers and sisters, of course, and they will never catch up with them, but they can learn to live quite fulfilled lives within structured circumstances. Since more and more group training centers are offering family-type living arrangements for these, they no longer have to live their lives secluded in homes or in state institutions. Living with their peer group allows them to compete within the scope of their capabilities and affords fellowship and social function at their mental level.

There is even reason to hope for the severely retarded, for special training developments over the past few years have raised this 3½ percent of the retarded population from the imbecile classification of the past decade to a group who can be taught to talk, contribute to self-maintenance, and care for personal needs. Although these often have accompanying physical handicaps, much progress has been made in helping them overcome their handicaps and helping them learn to live with them. While there is no present medical ability to make them normal, there is much that is being done to enable them to lead a life that is meaningful to them. They will need supervision all of their lives, but they need not be treated as "basket cases" for whom everything must be done by others. They are neither hopeless nor helpless. They are greatly limited; but so is a one-year-old child, and yet he can thoroughly enjoy life if he is properly trained and supervised.

It is the profoundly retarded who seem to be so hopeless, for they often have secondary physical handicaps and their motor development is very slow. But even among these 1½ percent of all M.R.s there is reason for renewed hope. It has been demonstrated that they can be taught some basic self-care skills and some communication skills. Furthermore, many of them can participate in highly structured work activities.

The accompanying chart is used in Hebron Home as a quick review for our new employees, for it lists, in condensed form, the developmental characteristics of each degree of retardation, thereby helping us to adjust our expectations for the residents in our home.

So there is reason for hope, for much more work is being done with the retarded than has been done in past years. But for the Christian parent of an M.R. there is even more reason to hope, for throughout the Scriptures Christ Jesus is spoken of as the object of our hope. Our hope is not in man and his limited abilities; our hope is in an unlimited God, for 1 Timothy 1:1 says, ". . . [the] Lord Jesus Christ, which is our hope."

At least three benefits accumulate in the life of a Christian who fills his heart with hope in the Lord Jesus.

First, he realizes that he need not be ashamed. Paul wrote, "And hope maketh not ashamed;

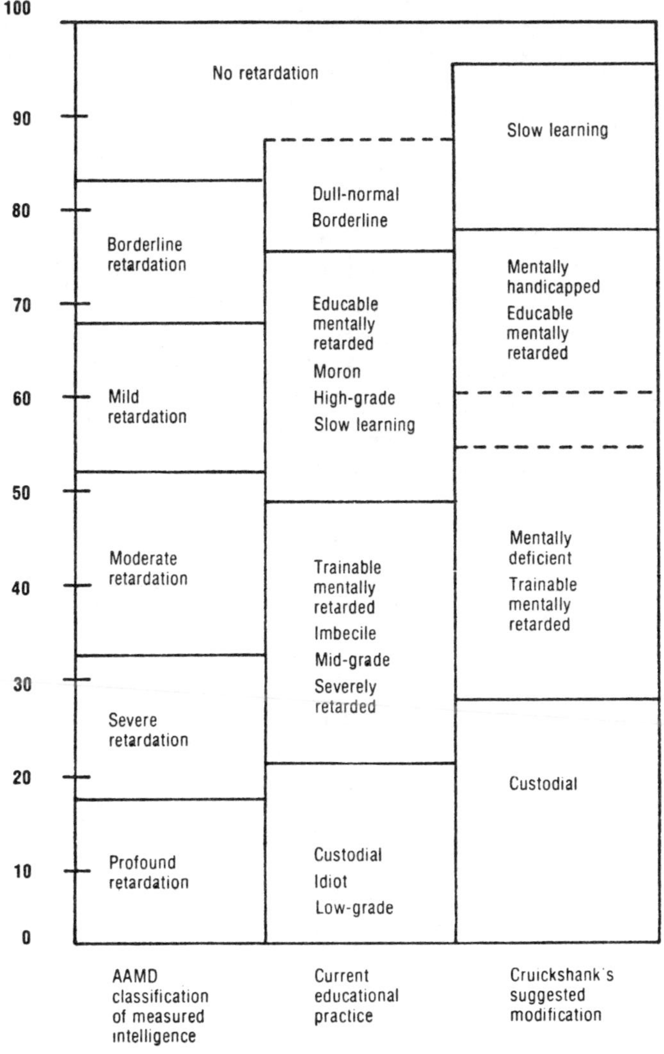

CLASSIFICATION OF THE RETARDED
Schematic Diagram of Three Systems
Based on Intelligence Test Scores
100
90
80
70
60
50
40
30
20
10
0
No retardation
Slow learning
Borderline retardation
Dull-normal
Borderline
Mentally handicapped
Educable mentally retarded
Mild retardation
Educable mentally retarded
Moron
High-grade
Slow learning
Moderate retardation
Trainable mentally retarded
Imbecile
Mid-grade
Severely retarded
Mentally deficient
Trainable mentally retarded
Severe retardation
Custodial
Profound retardation
Custodial
Idiot
Low-grade
AAMD classification of measured intelligence
Current educational practice
Cruickshank's suggested modification

because the love of God is shed abroad in our hearts by the Holy Ghost which is given unto us" (Romans 5:5); and, "According to my earnest expectation and my hope, that in nothing I shall be ashamed, but that with all boldness, as always, so now also Christ shall be magnified in my body, whether it be by life, or by death" (Philippians 1:20).

This was not written merely as Paul's testimony; it is an exhortation to all of us. Divine hope overcomes shame! None need hide his face because his child is not normal, for, if allowed to, God will flood the parent's heart with divine love for that "special child." Need we be ashamed of one we love so dearly? Isn't this "special child" a strong challenge to demonstrate a submissive will to God's provision, and to let Christ be magnified in the eyes of all who watch the developing relationship between the parents and this needy child? Many parents have testified to the special love that develops between them and this particularly needy child. This can be a powerful testimony to the many parents of apparently normal children who have failed to develop a love relationship in their homes.

Where there is hope there is love, and they will successfully overcome shame.

There is a second benefit to a life filled with hope in God. The Psalmist said, "Happy is he . . . whose hope is in the Lord his God" (Psalm 146:5). The coming of a retarded child into the home need not be the end of happiness unless the parents give up all hope. Hope and happiness are paired. One is the outgrowth of the other. The hope-filled person is a happy person, and the happy person is hopeful. Happiness is not totally keyed to present happenings; it is often rooted in a hope for better times. Many a young marriage has endured near-poverty as the partners started life together, and yet they had great happiness with nothing because they had great hopes for the future. Conversely, many a woman with virtually everything money can buy is totally unhappy because her marriage is breaking up and there seems to be no hope for the future.

God has mercifully given us hope to cushion the periods of harsh reality and to motivate us to happy endurance because we're convinced that the difficult place is only for a short season. Walking in dark places is made so much easier if we have a point of light toward which to walk. Hope is that shining light just ahead of us.

We're happy because we're hopeful. Even though our child will be limited during his "threescore years and ten" here on this earth, that is only the beginning of his life. Through a sharing of Christ's love we can bring that "special child" into a love relationship with Christ that will prepare him for complete fulfillment in eternity. Jesus taught us that "unless you turn and become like children, you will never enter the kingdom of heaven" (Matthew 18:3, RSV), and here we have one entrusted to our care who will maintain much of his childlike nature all through his life span. His faith will never be challenged by higher criticism, nor his love for God diluted by intellectualism. He may miss out on some of the benefits of higher education, although he probably won't truly know this, but he may be further ahead in spiritual faith than some of the rest of us.

When we view retardation as a physical thing we can rest assured that it affects only the span we call "time," for in eternity we will have new bodies—spiritual bodies—that will be absolutely perfect in every respect. So the Christian can accept retardation without losing his share of happiness, for his hope in the loving provision of the Lord becomes the source of his happiness.

There is a third function of hope that may well be more important than removing shame and imparting happiness. Paul wrote, ". . . we never forget that . . . the hope that you have in our Lord Jesus Christ means sheer dogged endurance in the life that you live before God, the Father of us all" (1 Thessalonians 1:3, Phillips).

"The hope . . . means sheer dogged endurance." The New International Version translates that phrase as ". . . and your endurance inspired by hope in our Lord Jesus Christ."

Any parent of a "special child" will testify to the need for "sheer dogged endurance." That child requires at least twice the time, attention, and financial investment for more than twice the period of time that normal children do. Patience wears thin. Strength gives out. There never seems to be enough hours in the day to get everything done. Personal goals and ambitions have to be set aside; the marriage relationship is often strained, and social engagements are severely curtailed. But the parents must not only continue to function; they must "endure to the end" (Matthew 10:22). Hope gives them that endurance. Hope inspires endurance. Hope inflames the heart until the harried parents can endure for another few hours or for another day. They are not on an endless treadmill; they have hope that they are actually making progress. They are not functioning in a state of shock, shame or sadness; they have hope, and that hope has superseded the shock with a settled assurance that God knows what is best for their lives. Furthermore, hope has replaced their shame with an overwhelming divine love, and hope has exchanged their sadness for happiness.

Let none take hope away from those God has seen fit to saddle with the responsibility of caring for the retarded. That hope is a divine enablement that prevents self-destruction. It is a source of courage, determination, and happiness. It compensates for many losses; it motivates to renewed efforts, and it invigorates in the midst of apparent failure.

But it is equally important that these chosen

few have the proper goal for their hopes, for a hope for the unattainable will end up in hopelessness. If we let Christ, not our personal dreams or ambitions, be the true source of our hopes, we will not be inspired for the unattainable, nor will we seek for too much too soon.

Hope, properly attuned to the circumstance, will get anyone through the most severe problems—even those encountered in retardation. Nothing is absolutely hopeless in the light of God and eternity. Paul taught, ". . . Christ in you, the hope of glory" (Colossians 1:27), so ". . . be not moved away from the hope of the gospel" (Colossians 1:23). Where there's life, there's hope, and "God hath given to us eternal life" (1 John 5:11).

"Christians, Receive Us"

The problem of retardation will not go away merely by ignoring it. Based on the 1977 estimated population of the United States (216,817,000), the 3 percent figure given us for the number of M.R.s in the United States would come to 6,504,510 persons. That is nearly twice the population of Israel, Ireland, or New Zealand. It is much larger than the populations of Albania, Zaire (Congo), Costa Rica, Guatemala, or Haiti. It is greater than many of the countries to which Americans traditionally send missionaries and missionary funds.

To simply state that 3 percent of America's population could be classified as retarded doesn't seem like much until the figure is extended to six and one-half million. But even that figure is not easily comprehended until we realize that only nine states in the United States had a population of over six million in the 1970 census. That means that there are more retarded people in the United States than there are residents in forty-one of our states.

To put it in an even more graphic perspective, there are more mentally retarded people in the United States than the total population of Washington, Oregon, Alaska and Hawaii put together. Actually, they almost equal the population of Florida. Furthermore, there is nothing at the present that would indicate that this number is getting smaller.

When we compare the number of churches, pastors, priests, and rabbis that are available to help the people of the forty-one states whose populations are less than the total number of retarded persons in the fifty states with the limited personnel available to counsel, guide, and encourage the M.R.s, it is totally disproportionate.

Certainly we are not suggesting that missionary funds should be diverted from foreign lands to help the M.R.s of America, nor would we place high value on building special churches for the retarded. But it does seem overdue for the churches of America to stop ignoring such a large segment of our population and open our arms to receive them. Over the past few years we have broken down many walls and barriers that have separated us. Doctrinal differences are being set aside in the interest of fellowship. Cultural and educational differences are being ignored for the sake of brotherhood. We have developed a tolerance that has enabled us to receive one another for what we are without despising each other for what we are not. Can't this also extend to the M.R.s of the community?

The M.R. needs to be received and accepted. He too has feelings and desperately needs to belong. He is aware of his limitations—far more aware than we are—but he is also aware of his abilities and of being a person. He wants and needs to be received as a person no matter how great his limitations. Although the M.R. may learn to expect rejection, he never gets used to it any more than we do. How often I have observed M.R. children dreading to go outside to play because of fear of rejection or mockery. Adults fear going to work lest they be totally shunned by other workers on the job, and all M.R.s generally hesitate to go to church because of the feeling of rejection they experience when they go.

Because the M.R. usually maintains a childlike quality in his life, he is often more capable of seeing through our sham and hypocritical relationships than we are. In Hebron Home we have observed a keen awareness of the difference between true and false. Although they may have mental deficiencies, the residents seem to be able to "read" sincerity and insincerity as rapidly as we can read a billboard. On more than one occasion after a visitor has left the home I have had residents say to me, "He said he loved us, but he didn't really mean it." They were usually right.

I have often marveled at how easily my brother Judson has moved from culture to culture as he has traveled throughout the world preaching and teaching. When I asked him his secret, he told me, "I asked a veteran missionary friend of mine, Edward Miller, how to relate to different cultures and religious heritages. He told me, 'Judson, just remember that different is not inferior.' From that time on I ceased viewing the different as inferior. It is merely different. This has enabled me to accept Christians of all cultures and religious heritages as my brothers and sisters in Christ Jesus. Once I have truly accepted them, it is easy to relate to them."

Shouldn't the same principle hold true in our association with those whose mental capacities are beneath ours? They are different, but not necessarily inferior, for what they may lack in mental prowess, they often make up for in a capacity to love and appreciate. Just as a man who was born without legs is different from us but is very much a person and capable of developing skills and abilities we will never acquire, so the person who was born with an underdeveloped mind is different but is very much a person and is capable of developing some areas of his life to a level equal if not superior to our level.

Even if the mental limitation is so great that the person is never able to develop great skills, he can still be received for what he is without being penalized for what he isn't.

When Paul wrote to the church at Rome he exhorted them, "Him that is weak in the faith receive ye" (Romans 14:1). If the church is to receive one whose faith is weak and whose doctrine may be faulty, surely the same principle applies to the one who is weak in his mental capacity. In chapter fifteen Paul prays, "Now the God of patience and consolation *grant you to be likeminded one toward another* according to Christ Jesus; that ye may with one mind and one mouth glorify God, even the Father of our Lord Jesus Christ," and then he pleads with them, "Wherefore *receive ye one another*, as Christ also received us to the glory of God" (Romans 15:5-7, emphasis added). The starting point of fellowship is "receive ye one another," for until we have done this, fellowship is impossible. Paul does not ask us to be like one another, only "likeminded one toward another," and the motivation for this command is "that ye may with one mind and one mouth glorify God."

We do this regularly in our churches. Our Sunday schools receive the children, thereby enabling them to glorify God with the adults. Special children's youth programs involve various age and maturity levels in the worship of God. In the process the entire family not only worships God, but each member aids in the maturity of the other members. The parents need the dreams and enthusiasm of the youth as much as the youth need the experience and wisdom of the elders. The children gain much instruction by the behavior of the older ones. They learn far more by example than by precept. Children make hero figures out of the teens, and the teens likewise pattern themselves after the young adults, who in turn idolize one of the older saints in the congregation.

But where will the M.R. find a hero figure if he is forever confined to his peer group? Our counselors at Hebron Home have long been aware of the value of a hero figure who is apart from the staff to become a model of an "adult" for the M.R.s. Even the intellectual genius needs a pattern for his life; how much more would a retarded person need a visual image to be a living visual aid to help him find normalization in his world? But there must be acceptance before the M.R. can identify with a hero image.

On August 2, 1978, the *Minneapolis Tribune* carried a column by Robert T. Smith in which he reported on a special performance of *The Wizard of Oz*. The special significance of the production of this longtime musical favorite was that it was performed entirely by retarded persons. "We want them to have a time to shine," said Jill Threlkeld, who directed the play. "They need to build confidence, to be applauded," she added.

All of us need to be applauded occasionally, but who applauds the M.R.s? They need not our pity or piety, but our praise. What they do may not seem like very much, but the difficulties they must overcome to do it deserve some acclaim. They certainly do not deserve being resented for their inabilities; they should at least be respected as persons and responded to positively.

Maybe we have placed too great an emphasis upon mental prowess in our technologically advanced society. We tend to downgrade anyone who cannot meet certain minimum mental levels. Rehabilitation counselors in Puerto Rico approach the problem of mental retardation with a much more realistic attitude. Many of their retarded clients possess physical problems that brought them to the counselors. Although diagnosis shows retardation, the counselor goes ahead and obtains the medical attention needed for his clients, and then finds jobs for them. It does not seem to matter that the client is retarded. If the client seems to be rather slow or stupid, the counselor simply fits him into a job opportunity where speed and intelligence are not necessary. They seem bent upon salvaging what is left, not criticizing what is absent.

The M.R. isn't asking to be received as an equal—only as a person. He knows he cannot compete with the rest of the world, but he feels he has a right to fit into it. He may not be capable of doing a problem in mathematics, but he may be one of the best and most faithful men on the assembly line. It has been our experience that, having learned some employment skills, most mentally retarded persons make good employees.

They are conscientious in their work and seldom cause disruption.

The primary goal which we set for each person is based on his learning ability and is beamed toward "normalization"; that is, to be able to function and participate in life as nearly as possible as do other persons. This includes working, schooling, all kinds of community activities, homemaking, and even marriage for some.

Many times the key to the successful turning of a person's negative responses to his environment into positive action is simply finding out where his natural abilities and talents lie. After that, some training, opportunity and acceptance transpose a useless life into a useful and meaningful one. The illustrations in several of the chapters of this book prove this point.

Through my years of working with the retarded I have come to recognize that if a person is to change his behavior, five basic requirements must exist:

1. He must want to improve.

2. He must recognize his own weaknesses.

3. He must work in a climate of acceptance and helpfulness.

4. He must have some help from someone who is interested and skilled.

5. He must have an opportunity to try out the ideas and skills he has learned.

It is likely that the home plus one or more of

the various agencies available to the retarded person have already handled the first two requirements, but the last three need our help. Whether we are parents, employers, pastors, Sunday school teachers, or active church members, there is much we can do to create a permissive climate and environment for the M.R.s. We can help them develop some skill and give them an opportunity to try it out. We can love them enough to receive them as persons, and can honestly praise their successes while overlooking their failures. Christ has done so for us; let's do the same for the M.R.

A life is far too priceless a thing to waste. If it must be lived with an underdeveloped mind, let it live! While their capacity to enjoy and appreciate life may be far beneath that of others, shouldn't they be allowed to enjoy their capabilities to the fullest? Through no fault of their own they have mental and often physical handicaps to plague them throughout their entire time on earth. They don't need the isolation of nonacceptance; they need the normalization of acceptance. It is Christian love—a quality that will accept the imperfect—that they need. We've received it from Christ; let's share it with them!

NOTES

[1]Harriet E. Blodgett, *Mentally Retarded Children: What Parents and Others Should Know* (Minneapolis, Minn.: University of Minnesota Press, 1971), p. 231.

[2]Blodgett, *Mentally Retarded Children: What Parents and Others Should Know*, pp. 32, 33.

[3]Beatrice Buckler, *Living With a Mentally Retarded Child: A Primer for Parents* (New York: Hawthorn Books, Inc., 1971), pp. 5, 6.

[4]Richard Koch, M.D., *Understanding the Mentally Retarded Child: A New Approach* (New York: Random House, 1974), p. 5.

[5]Professor Rick Heber, *Research of Personality Disorders*, (University of Oregon) p. 319.

[6]Judson Cornwall, *Let Us Abide* (Old Tappan, New Jersey: Fleming H. Revell Company, 1977), chapter 5.

[7]Jim Reese, "God Can Do Something Wonderful," *The Alliance Witness*, Sept. 1977, pp. 8-10.

[8]Mildred Copeland, Lana Ford, and Mary Salin, *Occupational Therapy for Mentally Retarded Children* (Baltimore, Md.: University Park Press, 1976), p. 43.

[9]Koch, *Understanding the Mentally Retarded Child*, p. 234.